FIRST EDITION

CREATIVE CONTENT AND MARKETING EDITOR: JULIE DROST LOKUN

ACQUISITION EDITOR: NICKI EASTON

For inquiries about this publication contact 847-361-9518

CROWN AND COMPASS/LINKTREE

"ALL YOU NEED IS 20 SECONDS OF UNBRIDLED COURAGE TO DO SOMETHING MAGNIFICENT."

-Julie Loken, Author, Boy Mama, Wife & Facilitator of Dreams

DEDICATION

STOP CHASING YOUR DREAMS & START BEING

Dedicated to my family, whose belief in me inspired me to Hustle Smarter.

<u>My Mother</u>-Who told me I could do anything and believed in me even when I stumbled.

<u>My Father</u>-Who led by example, an entrepreneur who made his dream a reality.

<u>My Husband</u>-Who allowed me the space to be creative and quirky and reinforced that I was on the path I was meant to be on.

<u>My Kids</u>-All four of my beautiful boys, whose curiosity and unabashed excitement reminds me of what is truly important.

HUSTLE SMART©
The Ultimate Guide On How to Start a Successful Online Coaching Business

⚜ Launching Your Coaching Business

The Hustle Smart Way

Are You Ready to Launch Your Coaching Business the Hustle Smart Way?

There is no competition in coaching. The more coaching businesses that penetrate the market the more this world is touched with strokes of brilliance. The key to your success as a coach is distinguishing your coaching brand, being consistent and leading with purpose. -**Julie Lokun**

You have your coaching certification-now what?

H ey Coach!

I promise you that your coaching dream is going to become a reality!

Building a coaching business that you love is a simple process. Now, when I say simple, I don't mean easy. As a coach myself, I understand that tipping point you are at. You have earned your coaching certifications and are eager to get your first client. Or, you desire to have a steady flow of clients and are yearning to quit your day job. You have credentialed yourself and are ready to jump in feet first.

Many of you reading this guidebook, are anxious to release the golden handcuffs of the corporate grind. Those nasty manacles keep you locked down in a job you dislike so you operate from a place of fear, not abundance. These fears may be rooted in the concern that you won't earn an income that is sufficient to support yourself or your family. This becomes a murky space to navigate.

It is time to start behaving like the coach you dream of becoming. Your mind is so powerful that when you start acting like a coach your beliefs follow suit. Afterall, your brain doesn't know the difference between a rehearsal and reality.

"You don't become what you want, you become what you believe." - **Henry David Thoreau**

YOUR LIFE AS A PROFESSIONAL COACH

As a coach, you will eventually have a consistent list of clients. If you manage your time, not only will you spend your days with these clients, your flexible schedule also provides freedom to enjoy time with your family. Your perfect work/life balance is within your grasp. However, many of my clients are in a rhythmic stall after they are credentialed to coach. Although they have a deep passion for making change, they are unsure of how to launch a thriving business. This happens because being an entrepreneur is a distinctively different skill set than that of being a coach.

The process of running a coaching business is skimmed over in most coaching credentialing courses. This scanty training leaves wide gaps in the glorious grind of building a business.

ENTER THE HUSTLE SMART GUIDE FOR COACHES

It is necessary to have an understanding of the tremendous work (or hustle) it takes to be one of the impactful coaching businesses that survives the exhilarating roller coaster ups and downs. It is crucial to understand the resilience needed to withstand economic fluctuations. This coaching business primer will guide you through the choppy waters of building and sustaining your coaching empire. If you are laser focused and ready to make a difference in both your life and the lives of your clients—read on! Today you will stop the wasteful hustling that leads to burnout. Today you will start Hustling Smart.

HUSTLE LIKE AN ENTREPRENEUR

What is a Hustle Smart Entrepreneur?

He/She is a coaching visionary that leads with a mission.

The HSE takes chances, seizes opportunities, and is a lifelong learner. The HSE does not quit their day job to launch their new business. The HSE strategically hustles while maintaining a consistent flow of income. The HSE squashes inner-doubt and laughs at the imposter syndrome. The HSE is unabashedly authentic and navigates their business with integrity. The HSE is resilient and learns from the fumbles along the way. And the HSE has an innate intelligence and hustles the smart way.

- Hustle Smart is a term I coined and use with my clients as bold verbiage to elicit their dream of capturing life's abundant riches.
- Hustle Smart is a resource to navigate that entrepreneurial whisper.
- Hustle Smart is the belief that using this method; you can take your idea and make it a thriving coaching business.
- Hustle Smart is a logical business blueprint that can lead you on a path to generational wealth in less than one year.

Now I share the practical method with you. This guidebook will teach you how to be an entrepreneur and take your coaching business to a new level.

⤸ LET THE HUSTLE BEGIN

MY JOURNEY AS A COACH

"Collect Experiences, Not Riches." - **Julie Lokun**

Even as a small girl, I was colored as a passionate, free-spirit. Family historians commented on my ability to embrace extraordinary opportunities. While meandering through various electrifying experiences over the years, I was met by an eclectic group of mentors who lit my soul on fire. These moments and people opened my heart to unique opportunities and quieted the bubbling murmurs of self-limiting thoughts.

As a girl, I looked at sparkly new ventures as a chance to meet new people and learn new things. I never factored "failure" or "what- ifs" into the equation. I understand that most people are not wired this way. I recognize that grounded, forward-focused people typically take an approach anchored with a well-thought-out blueprint. My gypsy-like navigation coupled with my "I can do anything" attitude met with stumbling blocks. However, these obstacles were not walls of resistance for me. They were the pages where I learned the most valuable lessons.

During my entrepreneurial exploration, sometimes I soared, and other times I plummeted. What has been constant in this entrepreneurial equation is my ability to get back up after setbacks, brush off my boots, and learn the lessons of my journey.

My fumbles along this path are now the teaching tools I impart to my coaching clients. Using a steady cadence of trial and error, I have created a functional roadmap that offers others the opportunity to revolutionize their ideas and ultimately monetize their service or product.

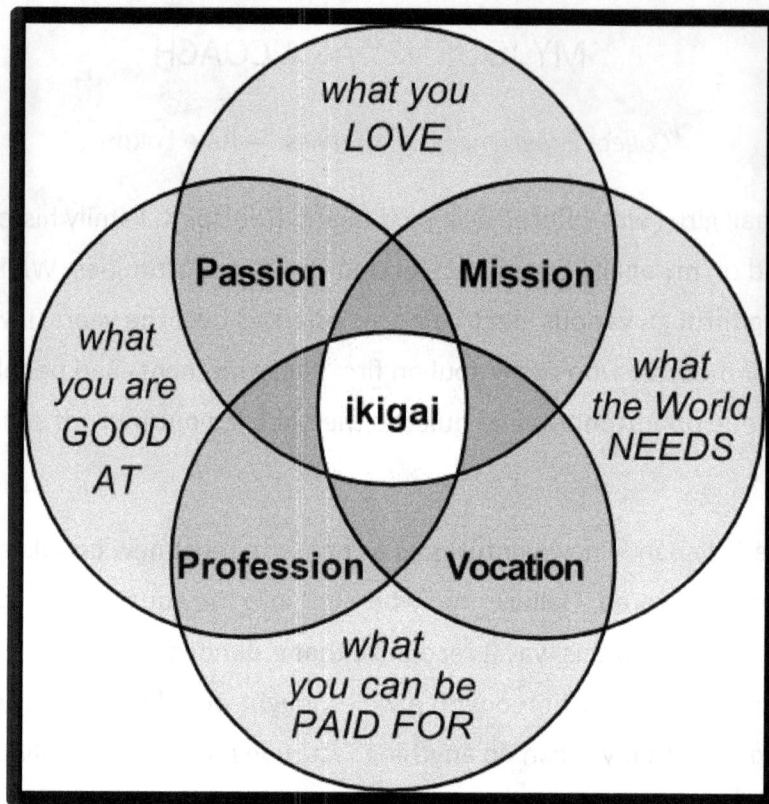

The image is a four-circle Venn diagram illustrating the concept of ikigai. The four overlapping circles are labeled: "what you LOVE", "what the World NEEDS", "what you can be PAID FOR", and "what you are GOOD AT". The overlapping regions are labeled Passion, Mission, Profession, and Vocation, with "ikigai" at the center.

My personal story began with a spark. I had just finished my Master's Certification in Life Coaching, and I wanted to practice this craft on a bigger scale. I recognized that coaching was my calling. Coaching was my Ikigai.

COACHING IS MY IKIGAI

What is "IKIGAI"? Ikigai is a Japanese concept that means "a reason for being." The word refers to having a direction or purpose in life that makes one's life worthwhile.

This mission, or Ikigai, is a primal calling from within, and I knew I was destined to live my life as a coach and lead the coaching industry with an authentic and innovative practice.

This entrepreneurial drive was sparked by a lightning bolt. The revelation hit me—I was an entrepreneur in the making. I needed to take this idea and make it a real, thriving business.

I approached this business idea with my usual figure-it-out-as-I-go-style. Spending countless hours basking in the dimly lit glow of my computer, I educated myself on launching a coaching business online.

Google became my teacher as I learned how to distinguish myself from the multitudes of other coaches that crowded the world wide web. Podcasts became my touchstone as I drank the Kool-Aid of the hustlers who went before me.

I dove deep into Facebook and Instagram to understand algorithms and the advertising cycle. I experimented with different forms of social media. And I made mistakes. One error was that I concluded that **Pinterest** was an out-of-date platform and that it reaped little benefits. I failed to realize that Pinterest is a search engine (not a social media platform) that can be as powerful as **Google**.

My path of educating myself landed in the bowels of **YouTube.** I also taught myself how to edit and make videos. With scrappy determination, I am proud to say I became a novice website designer. Perhaps my most satisfying accolade was when I taught myself how to create and market an online mastermind group. This became an extension of my practice and now boasts a nation-wide community of like-minded growth-seekers who meet weekly. The list of accomplishments I am proud of is lengthy.

To say that I was obsessed is an understatement. I spent days upon days lapping up every tip and trick to take my business to entrepreneurial prodigiousness. Through plucky ingenuity and a genuine belief in my skill set, my mission-based idea grew into a life-giving, full-time business in less than a year.

Does this sound impossible?

I guarantee that making your entrepreneurial dreams come true is possible. If your vision for your coaching business is born out of love, and is purpose-driven and not money-driven, you have the best chance of success. The bottom line is that because I was able to launch my coaching business successfully, I am doing what I am most passionate about—imparting wisdom and guiding people toward living the life they were meant to live.

YOU GOT THIS- Coach Jules

MODULE ONE:
HUSTLE SMART MINDSET

⚜ GETTING STARTED

You Are Certified and you Want to Coach Full Time.

WHAT'S NEXT?

I always ask myself, "why not" instead of "why."

This is a learned skill strengthened by trial and error. I wanted my legacy to be more than a woman with a passel of diplomas and a professional acumen of decent jobs. I wanted to do more than survive. I wanted to thrive.

I knew my purpose was to change the course of people's lives, but I didn't know how to go about it. I was plagued with self-doubt, insecurities and often played into the stereotype of the dumb blonde. These self-limiting beliefs were easy for me to fall back on until the discomfort of being mediocre outweighed the discomfort of my fear.

I implore you to take a look at the big picture. Take a look at the overarching vision of your life and ask yourself—*Am I actively pursuing my dreams? Or am I languishing in self-doubt?* If the answer is the latter, actively settling for what-is, try to articulate where and when someone told you that you were not worthy of an abundant life. Who told you that you were not worthy of living a big life? These voices from the past can be voices that originated from your self-doubt, a parent, or a teacher. Once you recognize these negative loops of self-talk, you can pause. Then, you repeat these messages, replacing them with a new voice that shouts, "Yes! I can"!

Remember- You aren't just a coach, you are an entrepreneur.

FIRST: ASSESS YOUR ENTREPRENEURIAL SKILL SET AND MINDSET

As you explore the idea of taking your idea to the next level, it is important to assess your commitment and drive. Do you have the attitude of an entrepreneur?

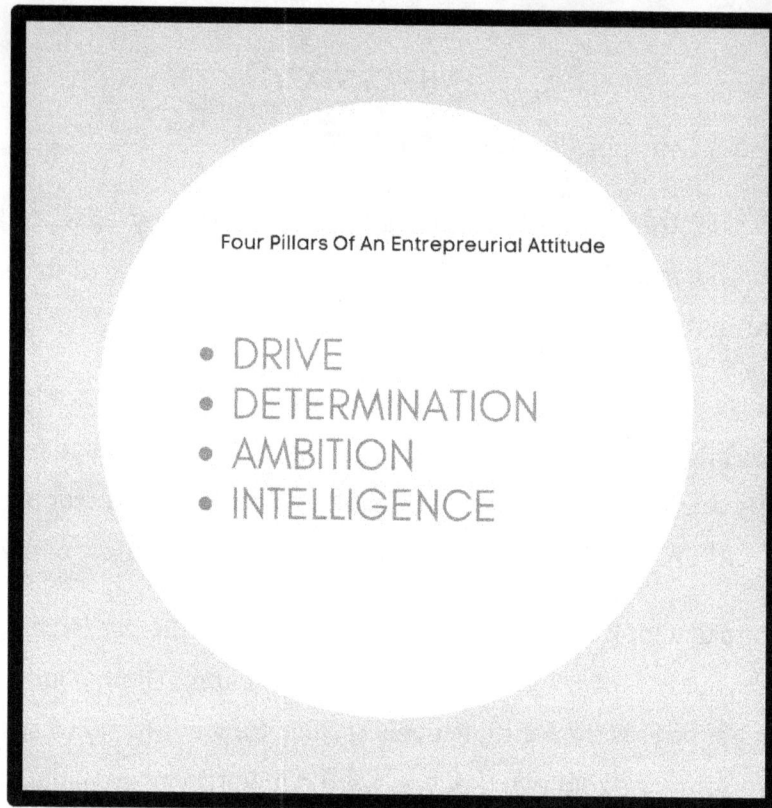

Four Pillars Of An Entrepreurial Attitude

- DRIVE
- DETERMINATION
- AMBITION
- INTELLIGENCE

Let's explore the four pillars of an entrepreneurial attitude.

DRIVE, DETERMINATION, AMBITION, INTELLIGENCE

This is the time to reflect.

→ Do you have a great idea?

→Do you have the grit to ride the wave of volatility?

→Are you flexible in thought yet steady in your approach to lead when times are lean?

Exercise: Start with these questions and journal your response below.

- What is your coaching gift or idea that you want to monetize?
- Do you have the aptitude to see this idea to fruition?
- Do you consider yourself a visionary?
- Do you have the mental space to open yourself to new ideas and innovation?

_____

_____

_____

_____

_____

_____

"Don't worry about being successful but work toward being significant, and the success will naturally follow." **-Oprah Winfrey**

WHAT IS INTELLIGENCE?

- Aptitude to gather interpret and prioritize information
- Commercial intellect
- Motivation
- Ability to scan business environments
- Ability to discern weaknesses, threats, opportunities, and trends.
- Confidence and courage to be decisive and assured (not cocky)
- Curiosity

*Exercise: Hustler Deep Dive

Be honest with yourself. What do you need to work on, and how can you work on your entrepreneurial intelligence?

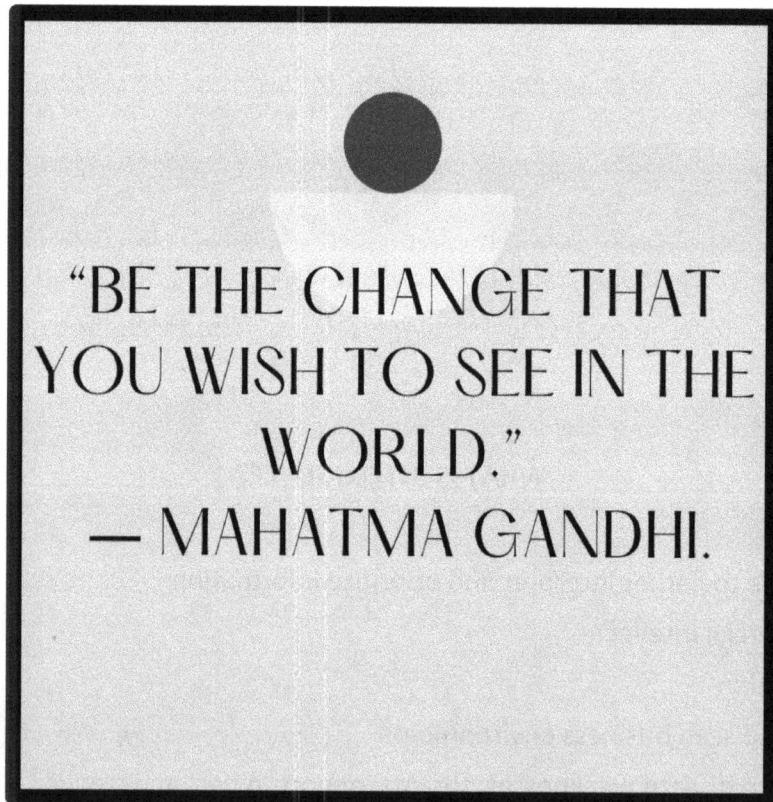

_____

_____

_____

_____

"BE THE CHANGE THAT YOU WISH TO SEE IN THE WORLD."
— MAHATMA GANDHI.

REALITY CHECK

Hustle with a Mission-Based Mind-Set Not a Money-Based Mindset

I am convinced that when you create a business simply to make money, you are setting yourself up for disappointment. When your idea isn't layered in a true passion or purpose, your clients will feel the disconnect. Your strength will falter in times of fiscal decline, and quite often, this will lead to burnout. When your venture is based on purpose, the energy you devote to creating a viable business is tapped from a well of dedicated momentum.

IMPLEMENTATION OF YOUR COACHING HUSTLE

While assessing your skills in regards to launching your product or service, ask yourself the following:

Do you have the:

- Communication aptitude for expressing yourself, your mission, and your idea clearly and concisely?
- Motivation to work extra hours and to go that extra mile to make your idea a mainstay in your audience's mind?
- Discipline to devote your energy to making your idea work?
- Persuasive leadership to direct your prospective audience and elicit the importance of your idea?
- Speed and Agility to get things done?

Exercise: Which of these skills do I possess? Which could I improve upon?

_____

_____

THE IMPORTANCE OF RESILIENCY

A Hustler has "the capacity to recover quickly from difficulties; toughness."

Resiliency is an essential component of structuring your idea and making it a reality. Often the road to fruition is laden with messy moments. When you are launching your coaching business, emotional and intellectual agility is necessary to adapt to changes. With a strong foundation of resilience, you can bounce back from failure and learn from the most important lesson an entrepreneur can encounter.

***Exercise:** Hustlers Thought Download

Do you have thick skin? How do you deal with failure?

_____

_____

_____

_____

_____

_____

As an entrepreneur, I have encountered situations that could have deterred me from my original mission. I have dealt with self-doubt, imposter syndrome, staffing issues, time management—just to name a few. I stayed true to my overarching vision of my business and embraced rethinking my approach.

THE HUSTLERS HARD ASK

WHAT IS THE *WHY* BEHIND YOUR COACHING BUSINESS

__Exercise:__ Do you have a business-driven mission? And if so, what is it? Who is your ideal client and how will you solve their problems?

_____

_____

_____

_____

_____

How can you shift your business mission from being money-driven to purpose-driven?

_____

_____

_____

What problem will you solve for your ideal client? What problem keeps your client up at night and how can you solve it?

_____

⚜ MISSION STATEMENT

Take time to craft a mission statement.

What is a mission statement? A mission statement, whether personal or professional, encapsulates the driving force behind your idea. This is essential to remind you of your overall mission and to unite your future team. A personal mission statement is designed to help you set goals that will drive change in your life. First, you must understand what drives you. This leads you to your principles and values and the fundamental truths about yourself. They are the fabric of who you are, whether you are consciously aware of them or not.

Coach Jules Mission Statement: To be a teacher that educates and empowers my clients to optimize their human potential.

*Exercise: Craft your Mission Statement below:

_____

_____

_____

_____

If you are having a hard time putting your mission statement into words, use my go-to guided exercise to prompt your mission statement with ease.

STUCK?

This is my go-to online tool that sparks mission statement creativity.

→ https://msb.franklincovey.com/

*Exercise: Postscript: After completing this exercise, tuck your mission statement away for a few days and circle back to the draft. How do you feel about your statement? What points still resonate? How can you condense this statement into a bite-size message?

The biggest fear new coaches tackle is self-doubt. Age, lack of finances, fear of rejection and lack of education often stall a new coach's career in its tracks. It is important to address these fears and check your mindset daily. Intentionally checking in with yourself and understanding the root of these fears is a healthy approach to moving forward with your business.

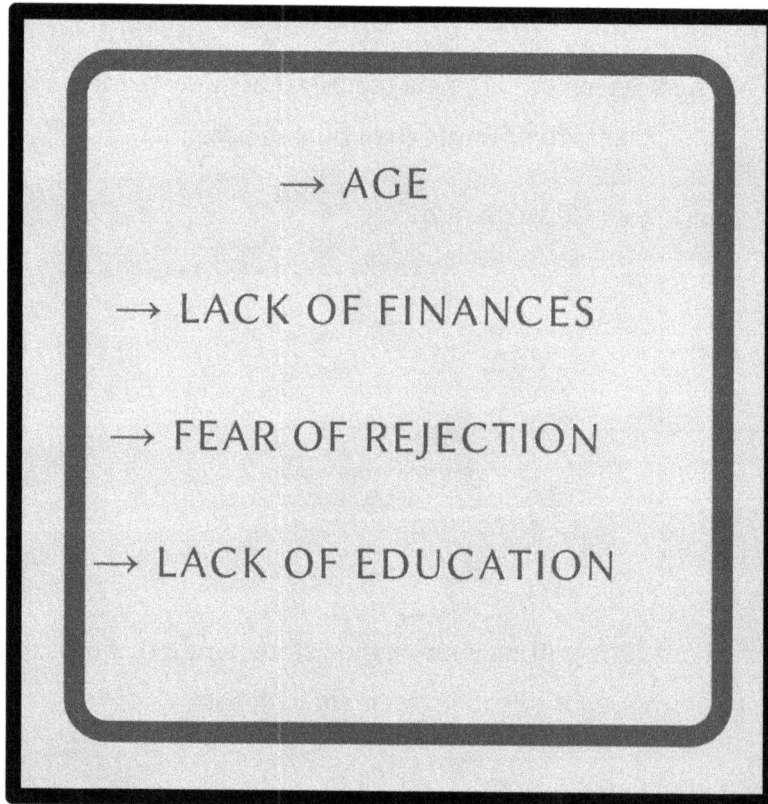

→ AGE

→ LACK OF FINANCES

→ FEAR OF REJECTION

→ LACK OF EDUCATION

MINDSET CHECK

Exercise: Overcoming a negative mindset. Once you have admitted it, you can control the fear of the unknown.

Write a list of your fears in regards to launching your business.

1.

2.

3.

4.

5.

Are these fears based in reality, or are they perceived fears of what may or may not happen?

1.

2.

3.

4.

5.

Of your original five fears, which ones can you cross off your list because they aren't reality-based?

_____

_____

_____

HUSTLE UNTIL YOUR HATERS ASK IF YOU ARE HIRING

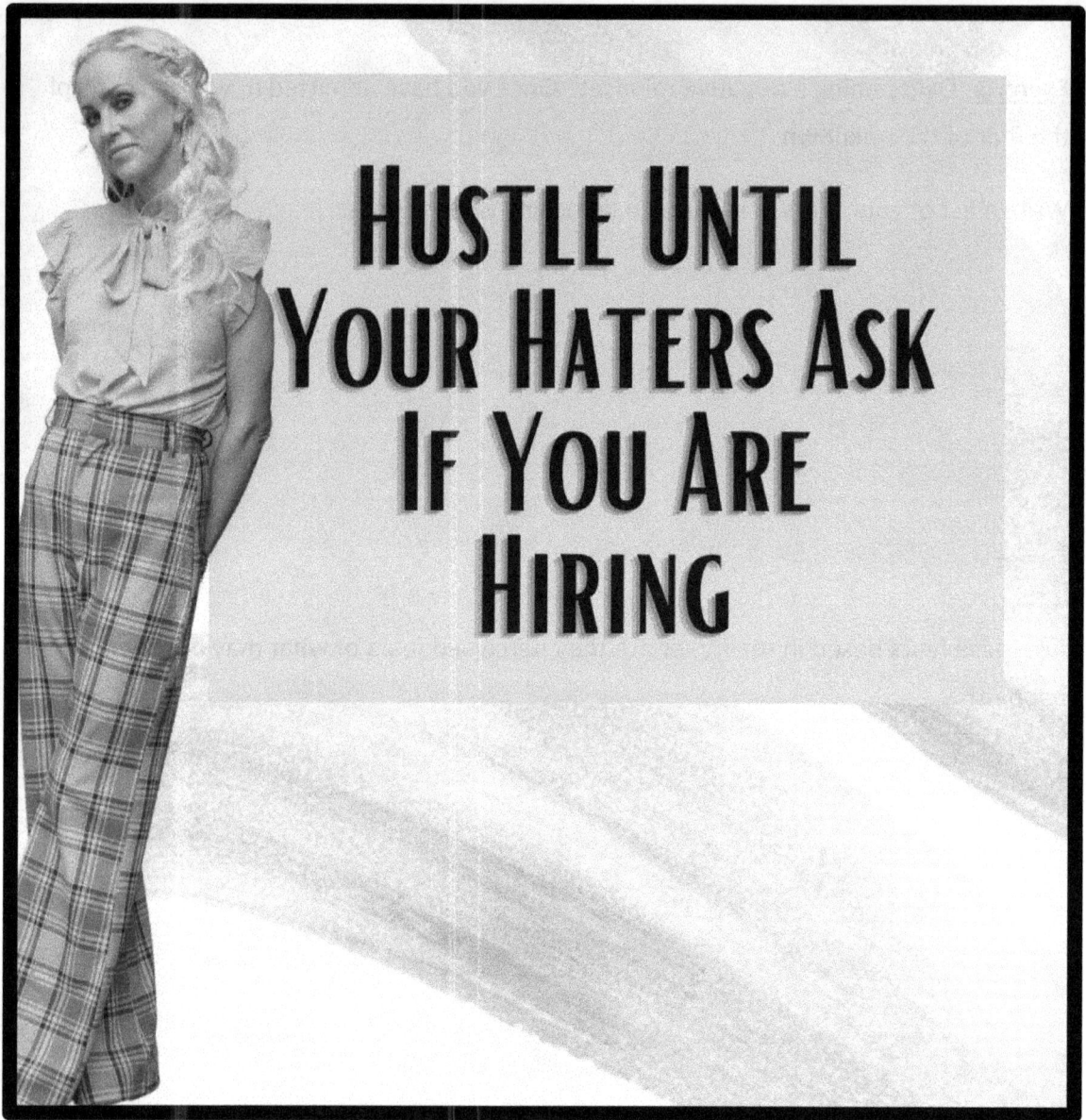

You have taken the time to understand your idea. You have a solid understanding of the grit and strength it takes to Hustle Smart.

Now it's time to put your idea to action.

"Never confuse motion with action." -**Benjamin Franklin**

SWOT ANALYSIS

Analyze your business idea with this tool. Look at projected strengths, weaknesses, opportunities, and threats. Use this tool quarterly as you progress in your business venture. It will help you assess your positioning and bring clarity to future projections.

Hustler's Tip: This is a great habit to practice quarterly.

Example of A Quarterly SWOT Analysis

YOUR BUSINESS (EXAMPLE)
QUARTERLY SWOT ANALYSIS

S

STRENGTHS

- Years of experience in brewing
- Established brand
- Products and packaging
- Stable financial performance

W

WEAKNESSES

- Appeal to other demographics
- Dependence on past practices
- Stagnant numbers
- Weak social media presence

O

OPPORTUNITIES

- Brand redesign can lead to consumer growth
- Learn more about craft beer and competitors
- Maintain quality of products but expand collection
- Look into a partnership with startup brands

T

THREATS

- Small businesses with craft beers
- Changing consumer preferences

WWW.JULIELOKUNCOACHING.COM

25

Hustle Smart

SWOT ANALYSIS

Strengths

Weaknesses

Opportunities

Threats

YOUR NEXT STEPS:

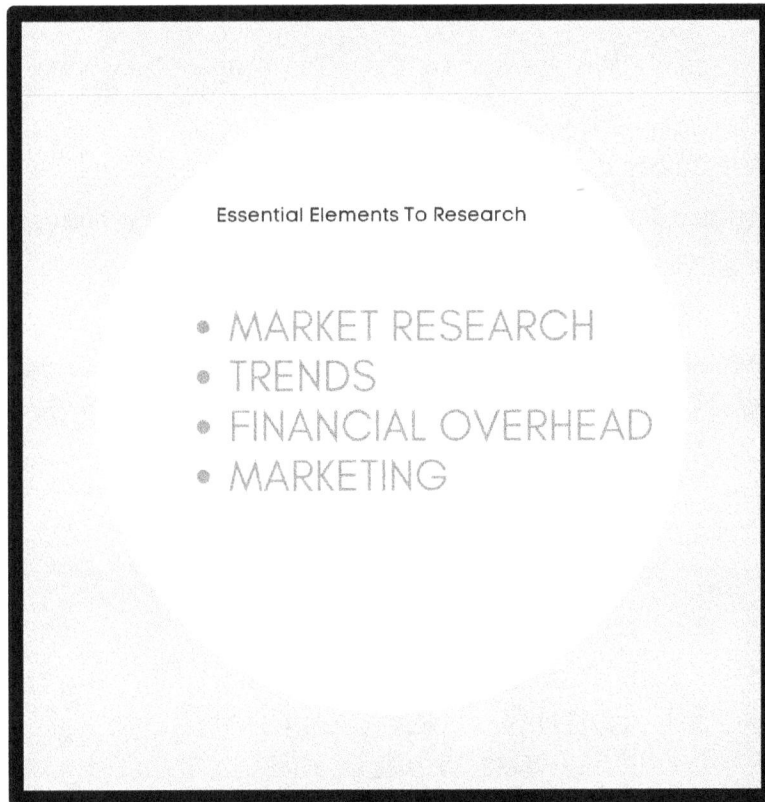

Essential Elements To Research

- MARKET RESEARCH
- TRENDS
- FINANCIAL OVERHEAD
- MARKETING

You have what it takes, the idea, the grit, and determination. You now have a clear understanding that there is the potential to monetize this business. And you know that businesses that are merely focused on the bottom line or making a quick buck end up as soul-sucking voids in an entrepreneurial venture.

DRUM ROLL PLEASE...

You are now at the intersection in your journey, where you must begin planning. Planning and research are essential in positioning yourself as a thought leader or expert in your industry. Without a comprehensive analysis of the market, your likelihood of success is diminished. Lack of research is the reason why so many start-ups fail.

LET'S TALK ABOUT RESEARCH

<u>Types of research:</u>

- Market Research-Who are your competitors. What are they doing right or wrong?
- Trends-What does the landscape of coaching look like?
- Cost overhead-Do you have the initial funds to launch your business?
- Marketing (Positioning)

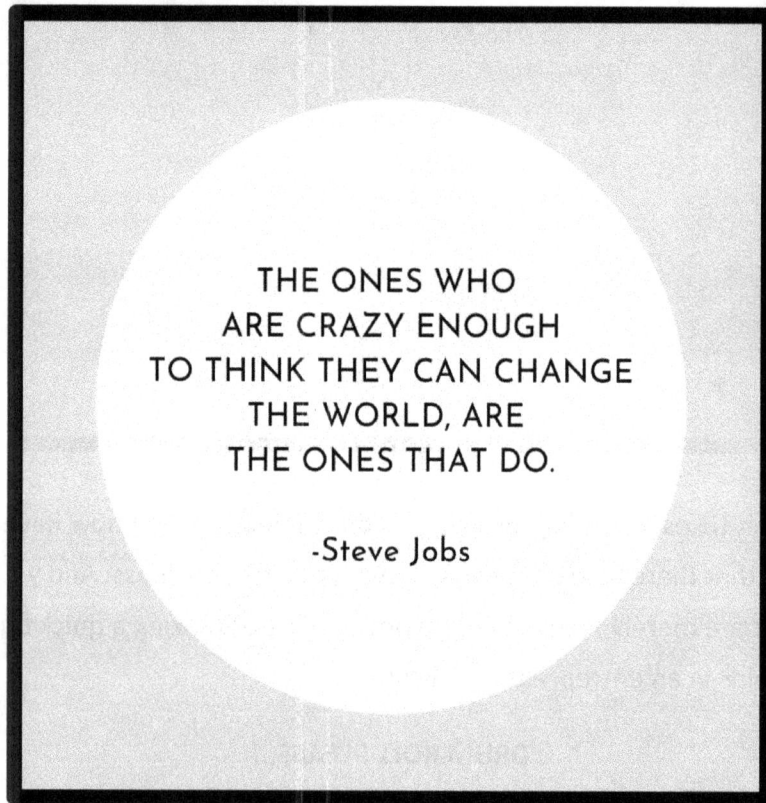

THE ONES WHO
ARE CRAZY ENOUGH
TO THINK THEY CAN CHANGE
THE WORLD, ARE
THE ONES THAT DO.

-Steve Jobs

NOTES:

_____

_____

The Hustler's Business Plan

*Exercise: Overview: This Business Plan will be the foundation of your professional mindset. Read and recite this daily.

My mission and purpose are to:

_____

_____

_____

My business is evolving into... (a team of... based in...) Be as detailed as possible:

_____

_____

_____

To achieve my business vision, I will:

Three-month Goal:

_____

_____

Six-month Goal:

_____

_____

Twelve-month Goal:

_____

_____

I am grateful I am able to solve this problem for my clientele:

_____

_____

My service or product allows my clients to:

_____

_____

Without my help, my clients will:

_____

_____

_____

As I focus on my work, I gain clarity that my services will better my clients' lives.

The most important action steps I need to take daily are:

#1:

_____

#2:

_____

#3:

_____

SECRETS TO SUCCESS

Here are a few tips to strengthen the foundation of your coaching business. I have learned the importance of asking for help. You are not an island. Reach out to those who have done this before you. Their wisdom will be invaluable.

Top Reasons Coaching Businesses Fail
- Inadequate Planning
- Lack Of Market Research
- Cash Flow
- Poor Management
- Staffing Issues
- Lack Of Competitive Edge
- Growth Is Too Fast

Get a mentor-A mentor in your field can be the secret weapon that elevates your business to the next level. Preferably find someone that is a few steps ahead of you in your entrepreneurial journey so they can provide you with their wisdom. Mentors often have a deep understanding of what works and what doesn't work and will guide and support your trajectory.

Hustle Smart Tip→You can sign up for free mentor matching at **www.score.org**. This is a valuable resource that provides a mentor in a similar industry. I can not emphasize this resource enough. My score mentor helped elevate my overall brand and put me in direct contact with VPs of large organizations, where I had the opportunity to pitch my executive coaching packages.

Understand Proximity-It is essential to create proximity to the industry you wish to position yourself in. For example, if you are a photographer, join networking groups, talk to other photographers, and offer up your expertise for free. The most important thing is to meet people.

NOTES:

_____

_____

_____

_____

_____

_____

_____

MODULE 2:

ARTICULATION + CREATION OF YOUR BUSINESS

CREATING A POWERFUL COACHING VOICE YOU LOVE

BRANDING

Branding is the essential element in creating a connection with your audience.

A BRAND CAN BE ANYTHING

We are used to thinking about brands in relation to companies and products. *(i.e The golden arches of McDonald's or or the simple logo of Apple).* But nowadays, anything can be a brand. Even as an individual, you have a personal brand.

So what is your personal brand? Whether you're known for your snaps, or you're still using a typewriter, you have a brand that exists both on and offline.

Luckily, there are great tools and resources to help you with the personal branding process. Use them to leave the right impression on people who look you up online.

The idea of personal/professional branding makes some people uncomfortable. But, if you don't take control of your personal brand online, you are missing out on opportunities and letting others control your narrative.

While the specific circumstances and goals vary by entrepreneur, the overall concepts and process are still applicable to every entrepreneur.

PERSONAL BRANDING

and why this matters

"Without a story, you are just an inanimate object. A story elicits a connection with your audience and has the power to bring you and your vision alive"- **Julie Lokun**

It just so happens that personal branding is an obsession of mine. Sometimes I get the obligatory eye roll when I present the question, "What is your personal brand"? I am met with responses such as, "I don't need personal branding" or "This is an uncomfortable space. It seems so narcissistic". The truth of the matter is that if you don't control your brand, others will. People make judgments based on how you present yourself; therefore, you create a personal brand just by existing.

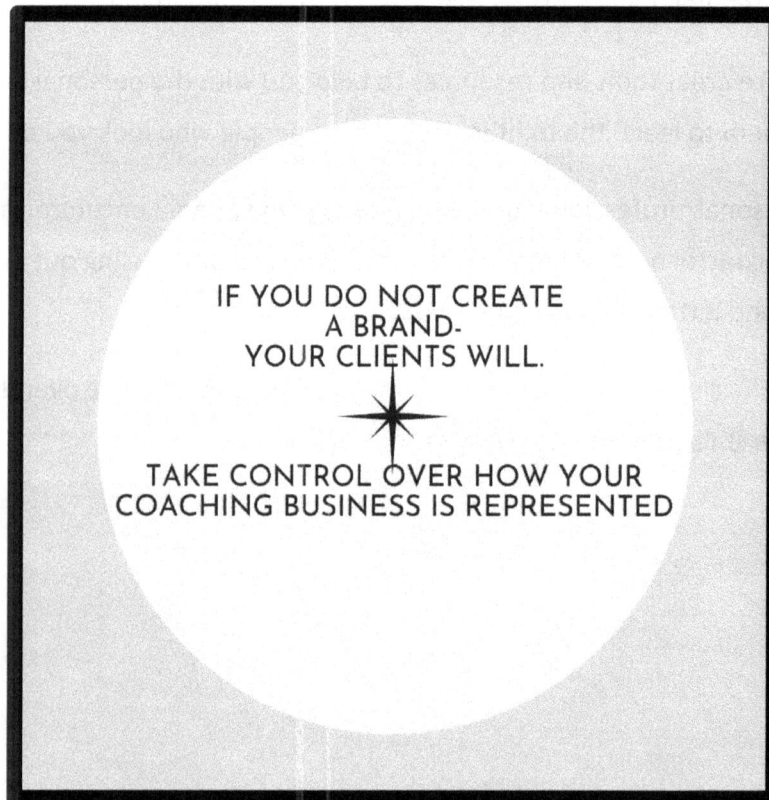

IF YOU DO NOT CREATE
A BRAND-
YOUR CLIENTS WILL.

TAKE CONTROL OVER HOW YOUR
COACHING BUSINESS IS REPRESENTED

Personal branding is an essential cog of the professional branding machine and is the essence of who you are as an entrepreneur. By embracing your brand, you live this brand intrinsically and extrinsically. Your core values and beliefs are directly reflected in how you present and manage your professional identity. So, personal branding and professional branding are one and the same.

To further clarify, branding is an illustrative description of what you, as a human, represent. Do you represent integrity? Are you creative? Maybe you have a bohemian heart? The list is endless.

*__Exercise:__ Take a minute to pause and write down three cornerstone phrases that represent you.

1.

2.

3.

Analyze these key phrases and articulate how they distinguish you in a personal and professional realm.

YOUR BRANDING STORY

Sharing a story with your audience is key in connecting with any demographic. Anecdotes personalize the experience and garner trust and loyalty.

*Exercise: What is your story? What led you to this point? How has your product or service played a pivotal role in making your life better?

_____

_____

_____

_____

_____

_____

_____

How can you incorporate your story into your branding and marketing?

_____

_____

_____

_____

1. Conduct effective market research. Who are your competitors? What do you like and dislike about their brand?

2. Before making significant branding efforts, you will first have to answer a few key questions. Are customers aware of your brand? How can you authentically express your brand to connect with your target audience?

3. Focus on a unique value proposition. Your brand is your promise to the customer. (Fill in the blank).

4. Choose a brand name that delivers your message clearly. Once you have identified your customers' needs and desires and have come up with products to meet them, it's time to clearly articulate your service to help solve their problem.

5. Create an emotional connection. Psychologists have found that 90% of communication is non-verbal. How will you relay your message visually?

6. Deliver consistent communications. Once a company has developed an effective brand and corporate identity strategy, it must be implemented consistently through every "point of contact" with customers. Brainstorm various points of contact that your potential client will engage with your branding.

MY BRANDING STORY

The Birth of Crown + Compass

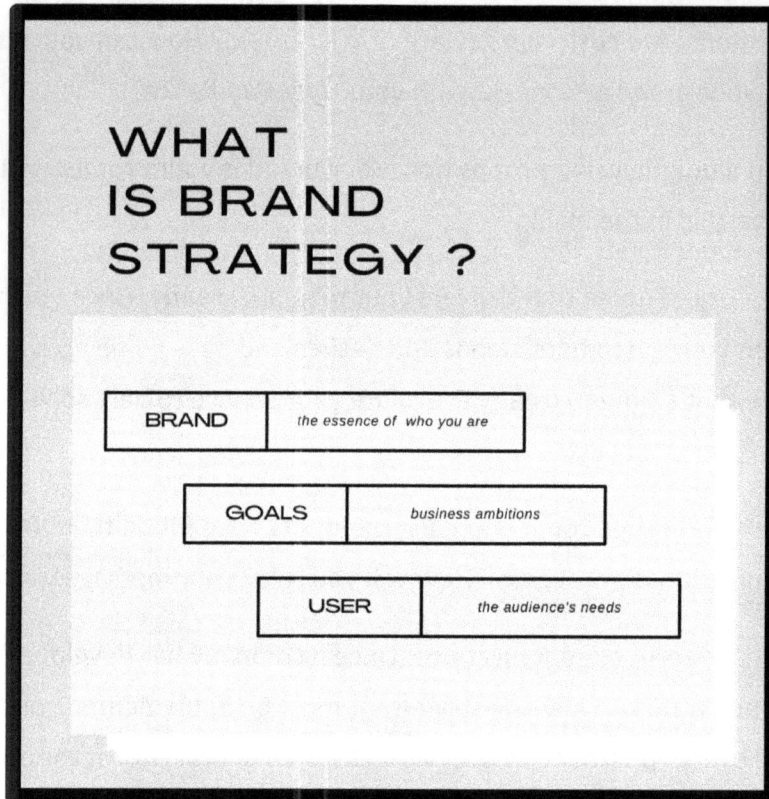

WHAT IS BRAND STRATEGY ?

BRAND	the essence of who you are

GOALS	business ambitions

USER	the audience's needs

When I decided to launch my coaching program online, I knew I wanted to distinguish myself amongst the multitude of other coaches that inhabit the online space. Let's face it; life coaches are a dime a dozen. Not to diminish the coaching profession, as we figuratively have locked arms to uplift our fellow humans. But, quite honestly, this unregulated industry allows every Tom, Dick, and Mary to hang a sign on their door and magically transform themselves into a coach. I knew I was different. I knew I brought to the table a legacy of advocacy and a pedigree of higher education that set me apart from the rest. However, screaming these hard facts to the world wasn't enough.

KNOW YOUR AUDIENCE

Understand the problem you will solve for this collective group of potential clients/customers.

I started my branding journey by focusing on my potential clients. The trendy name that is assigned to this process is understanding your "brand avatar". What I knew for certain is that I had to provide significant value to their lives. This is when I grabbed a nubby number 2 pencil and scratch paper and started to brainstorm. Who do I connect with in my life? Who do I, with casual ease, attract to my circle? I knew, fairly quickly, that I had the ability to foster profound relationships with women and teenage girls. (I apologize to Jeff, Larry, Josh, and the handful of evolved guys that "get" me). But in all sincerity, I knew my superpower was connecting with women and raising their vibrational energies.

I also had a clear vision of how I could add value to their lives by redirecting their patterns and creating a space where they could elevate their self-esteem. I also recognized I could distinguish myself as a coach because I offered a background in journalism and law. My strength is my educational foundation, and I relished with unabashed glee when potential clients were surprised by these degrees in law, journalism, and life coaching.

What distinguishes my brand is my ability to foster an authentic connection with my clientele and instill real tools to elevate their careers, relationships, and overall wellness.

The Branding Brainstorm

Inside my branding brain

★ I help my clients remove their proverbial tarnished crown from atop their heads. I assist them as they polish it and reposition it, so it shines for all to see.

↓

★ MY BRAND, Crown & Compass, elicits the feeling of how I facilitate client's dreams by anointing and pointing them towards a life of peak performance.

↓

So-> I <u>ANOINT</u> them with confidence and <u>POINT</u> them in the right direction.

↓

= MY BRAND: ANOINT + POINT | CROWN & COMPASS COACHING

NOTES:

_____

_____

_____

_____

YOUR TURN: Hustler's Brainstorm

*Exercise: Articulate three words that conceptualize your personal values. These are values that you present simultaneously in your personal and professional life.

i.e., passionate, empathetic, and creative.

1.

2.

3.

How can you elicit these three Core Concepts to an audience?

_____

How can you visually convey these concepts to your audience?

_____

10 Criteria For A Smart Coaching Brand Name

- ☐ Instantly conveys what my business relates to
- ☐ Sparks the interest of my target audience
- ☐ Is simple to pronounce and spell
- ☐ Is easy to remember and recall
- ☐ Is distinct and unique from competitors
- ☐ Has no risky copyright or trademark issues
- ☐ Website domain is available, ideally dot com
- ☐ Social media handles are available
- ☐ Reflects my brand's mood and personality
- ☐ Will remain relevant as my business evolves

Positioning Your Brand

The Hustle Smart Guide to Creating an Online Presence and Audience-Targeted Marketing

The demand for an online presence is non-negotiable in launching your business. If you are a staunch objector to Facebook, Instagram, Pinterest, and similar platforms, I urge you to reconsider. Taking time to understand the power of social media engagement is a necessary evil when unleashing your brand onto the world.

The Power of Google

- Try Googling Yourself. What pops up? Your future client will very likely Google you to understand your reputation. What do you want your clients to see?
- Attaching your "brand" to Social Media Platforms will help you get "seen" on Google. Because Facebook and the like are a powerful presence on Google, having social media accounts will boost your rankings on Google and other search engines.

Google My Business: Google My Business is a free platform that allows businesses to create their profiles, entering important info such as their location, operating hours, official website, and products/services they offer.

All this info appears in a small section at the top of the search engine results pages (SERPs).

Suppose you own a law firm in the USA, and you've listed your location on your GMB. Now, if somebody searches the keyword "lawyers in USA" on Google, they'll see a list of websites that have high SEO scores for this particular keyword.

Plus, they'll also see a list of local businesses at the top of the SERP. These results are the GMB listings of relevant local businesses. As you can see in the image below, the searcher will also be shown a map of the area with the top listings highlighted.

From a marketing research standpoint, the Google My Business app will provide essential data about your target demographic. By utilizing this app, you will be able to see a surplus of valuable information including the general age, gender, and location of the people viewing your ad. In addition, you can have a better understanding of what this demographic is looking for based on the search terms used to find your ad. When considering marketing research, Google My Business could be a possible one-stop-shop, providing a plethora of information, and containing it all in a single convenient space.

THE POWER OF PHOTOGRAPHY

We live in a visual society. The short-attention span of consumers lends itself to the importance of creating a visually appealing brand. As a coach, you are your brand.

Prior to establishing a foothold on these social media platforms and launching a marketing campaign, you will need to have a cohesive "look" that is an extension of your brand's message.

More Tips:

- Use the same filter for all your photos
- Keep the photos simple
- Include people in your photographs. Photos of People=More Interest
- If you are taking photos by yourself, use portrait mode on your phone
- Hire a novice or a friend with a good camera to take pictures of you
- Have a plan. Sketch out your ideas for your photos and ensure that your product/service is adequately represented
- Hire a professional photographer
- Be creative and have fun
- Use natural lighting
- Create a story
- Create a call-to-action
- Barter with photographers
- Use Stock Photos (Unsplash, Pixabay)

CREATING AN ONLINE PRESENCE

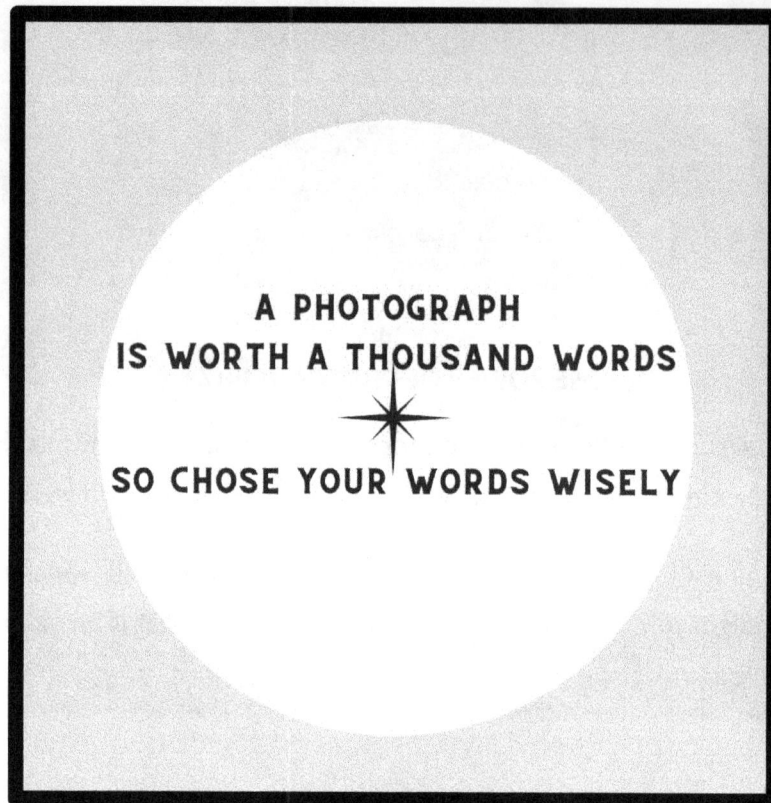

A PHOTOGRAPH
IS WORTH A THOUSAND WORDS

SO CHOSE YOUR WORDS WISELY

The marketing journey is complex and ever-evolving. The topic of online marketing will be covered in-depth later in this guidebook.

The Short List

- ★ A Branded Website
- ★ Facebook Business
- ★ Facebook Lives
- ★ Email List
- ★ Your Reputation
- ★ Instagram
- ★ Instagram Live
- ★ Clubhouse
- ★ Pinterest
- ★ Press Releases
- ★ Podcasts (court podcasts to be a guest)
- ★ Community Involvement
- ★ Networking
- ★ A website (WordPress, Wix, or Shopify)
- ★ Google Business
- ★ Google Ads
- ★ YouTube Channel
- ★ Partnerships With Other Companies
- ★ Media (features on your service/ product)
- ★ SEO Management (Search Engine Optimization)
- ★ Etsy Shop
- ★ Ebay
- ★ Online Course Creation
- ★ Blogging
- ★ TikTok
- ★ Linktree

⚜ FINANCING YOUR COACHING HUSTLE

This is where the real meat of your business begins or ends. How much are you going to need to finance your business? Where will these funds come from? Practice forecasting possible costs. This chart will provide a framework for estimating future expenditures. Your coaching business doesn't have to be an expensive venture at first. However, I believe you have to spend money to make money.

Monthly
BUDGET

Month:

ITEM	BUDGET	SPENT	PLAN	REMAINS

TOTAL:

ITEM	BUDGET	SPENT	PLAN	REMAINS

TOTAL:

ITEM	BUDGET	SPENT	PLAN	REMAINS

TOTAL:

Money is an expression of energy and we use it to support our life. Consciousness is the awareness and internal knowing of thoughts, feelings and experiences. When money is earned, spent, saved and given consciously, it reflects what we value most. It becomes an intuitive gauge for who we are, what we stand for, and where we are headed.

WAYS TO FUND YOUR BUSINESS VENTURE

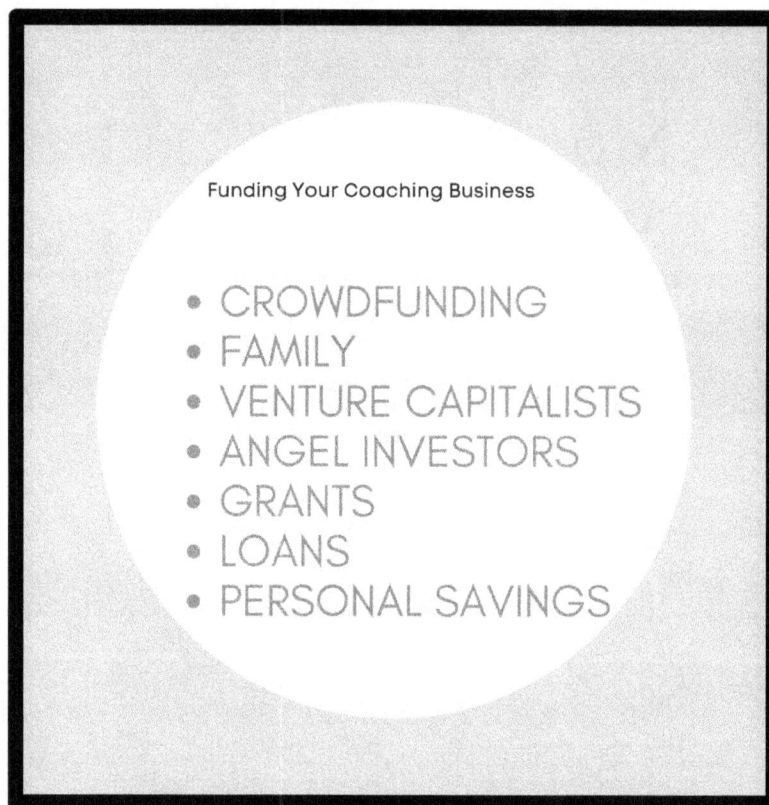

Funding Your Coaching Business

- CROWDFUNDING
- FAMILY
- VENTURE CAPITALISTS
- ANGEL INVESTORS
- GRANTS
- LOANS
- PERSONAL SAVINGS

If you are looking outside of yourself for start-up capital, you will need to put together a polished pitch for your investors.

Find the Right Investor-For a lot of founders, a pitch starts the moment you shake hands with an investor. Confidence in yourself and your idea will create an atmosphere attractive to potential investors.

Prepare Your Pitch Deck-Once you've found the right investor, it's time to start preparing. Create a short yet powerful presentation. Get your investors excited about your idea. (Think **Shark Tank)**

Tell Your Story-The point of a pitch is to inspire and excite, not put people to sleep. A personal anecdote woven into your pitch helps you make a connection with investors.

Nail Down the Details-Arguably, the most important thing you can do in a pitch meeting is to talk about the nuts and bolts of your operation. Do your research! Understand net profits. Explain marketing strategies. The bottom line is that your audience wants to understand the return on their investment.

Explain How You Will Solve The Problem-Clearly detail how you are uniquely qualified to solve the problem your potential clients face.

↓ Legalities

The Nuts and Bolts of Protecting You and Your Coaching Business

1. **Always Use Written Contracts-** (Avoid Oral Contracts) I have heard this question before, "Is an oral contract enforceable?" Yes, it is, but try to prove an oral contract in court! It is always best to CYA or Cover Your Ass. Even if it is an email or pieces of paper, you need to get everything down in writing. Have a "meeting of the minds" documented, so your project isn't sabotaged by someone's selective memory. Again, even an email between parties detailing what you both agreed to is better than nothing!

2. **Properly Categorize Workers-** (Independent Contractors Vs. Employees) Properly categorize your workers. There is a common misconception that business owners don't have to pay taxes on independent contractors. In reality, if you have a contractor acting as an employee, then they are an EMPLOYEE. The law will come down on you hard if you miscategorize a worker. It makes sense to do it the right way from the start and to avoid problems. I have seen several companies go out of business because they miscategorized workers. With the help of an opportunistic attorney, disgruntled workers won a Labor Board hearing, which classified the workers as employees and awarded missed mealtime and overtime pay. If you haven't been paying your workers properly, you have to pay penalties. Additionally, you may have to pay legal fees to defend against the lawsuit you will probably lose. A simple, inexpensive way to protect yourself from an employee lawsuit is by putting together a well-written and **comprehensive employee handbook.**

3. **Register Domain Names For Your Business-** (Names that Identify Your Business Brand) Register a few domain names that contain the name of the brand that you are trying to build. There is nothing worse than building a brand and finding out that a cyber squatter has bought your name and plans to extort you for a large amount of money before he or she turns it over. Be proactive. Register and maintain those domain names early. Try **www.godaddy.com or www.wix.com.**

4. **Register Your Trademark-**A trademark is the legal basis of any brand. It is the logo or the name associated with the product or service you are offering. Registering your trademark protects you from having no recourse if someone uses a similar mark for the same product or service without your permission. Initially, safeguarding your brand may not be a big concern, but the point of all your work is to one day be successful and build a brand. When that happens, then there will be people coming out of the woodwork trying to associate themselves with your brand. Also, note that there is a way that you can reserve your trademark while you are building your brand. That is a pretty smart way to start because, initially, you may not have the evidence needed to secure a trademark registration.

5. **Create an Entity-**The number one legal step you should consider when setting up a new business is creating an entity. That means forming a limited liability company (LLC) or incorporating (forming a corporation) for your business. The main reason for this is that you want to keep things separate. Always keep your personal assets separate from your business assets. Imagine someone sues you for a business matter, and they end up winning a judgment against your business and you personally. They could collect from your personal assets, like your bank accounts, home, car, etc. It's one thing to lose business assets in a lawsuit, but it's much more devastating if you lose personal assets. That could affect your personal and family life. You don't want a judgment holder from a business lawsuit to be able to collect from your personal assets, and vice versa. Check out **Legal Zoom**. This is a fast and easy way to create an LLC for your business.

6. **Business Insurance-**My parents believed in over-insuring to prevent future problems. So, I would be remiss in not mentioning that a well-oiled business plan includes insuring yourself against potential lawsuits.

If you do not feel comfortable with creating and implementing these legal documents, I suggest you hire an attorney. If you don't have the funds to retain an attorney, I suggest trying Legal Zoom. Legal Zoom is an affordable online tool that creates and files legal documents on your behalf. www.legalzoom.com

NOTES:

_____

_____

_____

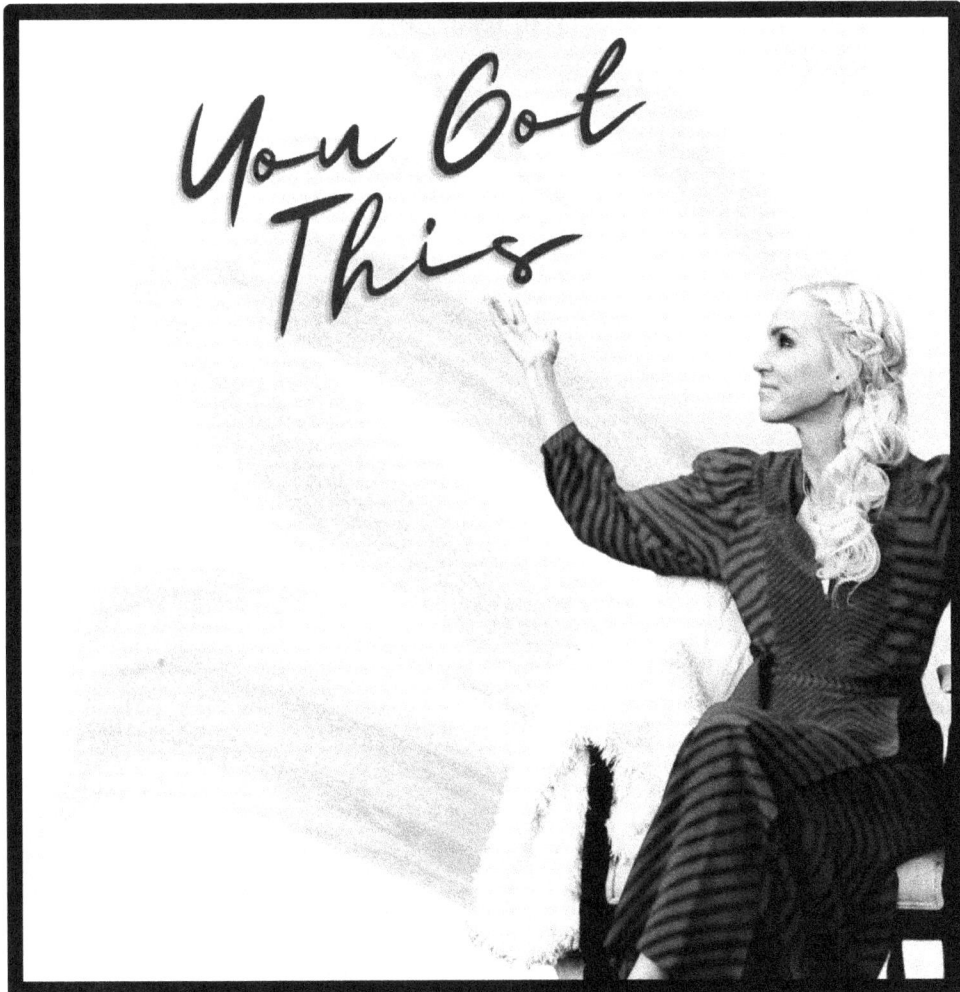

MODULE 3:

VISIBILITY OF THE COACHING BUSINESS YOU LOVE

GET READY TO LAUNCH THIS BUSINESS YOU LOVE

The Hustler's Legendary Launch

Congratulations Coach! You have a firm foundation on which to build a thriving coaching business. You have clarity in terms of what your business will look like, and you are confident in your ability to deliver a service or product that will most likely change the world. So now what? How will you attract paying clients who will pay for the commodity that you offer?

Many voices flood the internet, telling you how to land the sale. If you Google topics on marketing, your screen will flood with other businesses trying to make the sale. The overwhelming information contains marketing funnels, marketing campaigns, and similar calls to action that infuse brand awareness. These tools have their place. However, if these funnels and campaigns all worked, everyone would be a millionaire.

WHAT WORKS

There is no formulaic equation that can concretely predict monetary abundance. The time-tested approach begins with making a connection with future customers and rewriting their stories. This may sound vague or like gibberish, but we tell ourselves stories all day long. We tell ourselves that we need a particular beauty product or that we need to strive to be the CEO of a specific company. These stories tell us what we think we need and want. They can be stopped in their tracks when your powerful connection alters how a customer thinks about his or her story.

When potential clients understand that their story includes your product or service, they rewrite their experience, and the neuroplasticity of their brain changes.

First, understand your audience. Research to understand where this demographic spends most of their time. Are they on Instagram, or are they driving on a freeway daily, passing a display of billboards that often catches their eye? Once you have ascertained clarity about where your audience spends most of their time, you will then embark on the first pillar of building your business. The first step in connecting with this demographic is to build visibility.

THE FOUR PILLARS OF MONITIZING A COACHING BUSINESS YOU LOVE

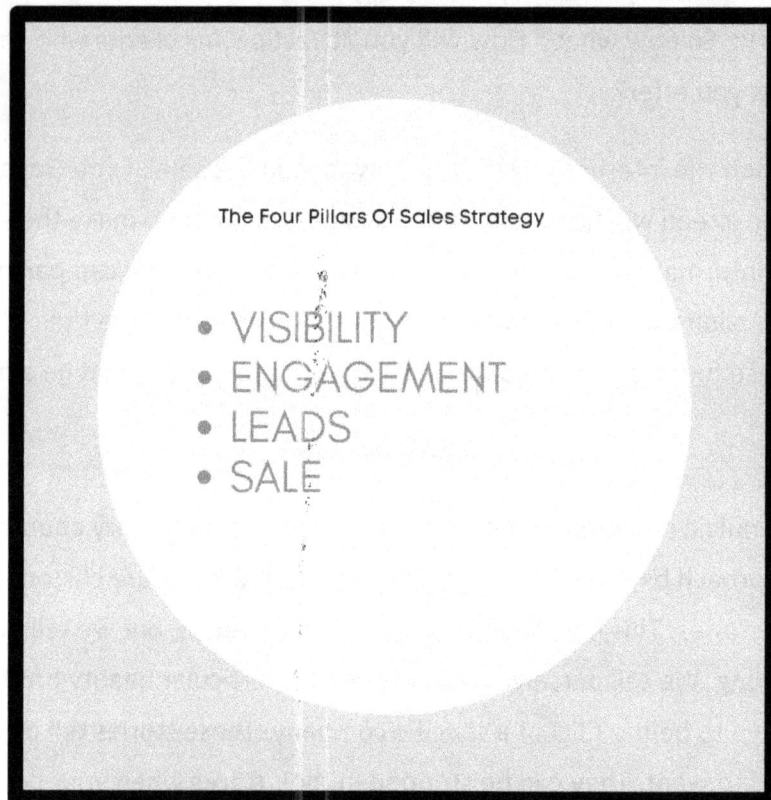

The Four Pillars Of Sales Strategy

- VISIBILITY
- ENGAGEMENT
- LEADS
- SALE

I will focus primarily on the first pillar, visibility. Visibility is the cornerstone of making your brand a powerful presence, which ultimately leads to closing the deal. Visibility is where you build a reputation and relay protocol about how your service or product is an agent for change.

Visibility is where the muscle of your hustle flexes. It draws upon a consistent flow of quality content and your ability to tap into a deep reservoir of resilience. Without visibility, you won't get the leads that materialize into a sale.

Visibility is everything.

If you start with the *land-a-sale mindset,* you ceremoniously extinguish the foundational element that creates a long-lasting, economy proof brand that will leave a stamp on your professional legacy.

The Importance of your story

The topic of visibility is not impactful without the inclusion of your own personal story. The practice of coaching creates an intimate relationship with clients.

THE HUSTLE SMART SECRET SAUCE

Harnessing the Power of Visibility-Visibility Is Key To Growing and Scaling Your Coaching Business.

Once you have a clear understanding of where your audience spends most of their time, you can get the creative juices flowing and reach your audience in unexpected ways. You can reach people through different avenues without the intention of making a sale. Instead, you will extend your brand presence by affiliating yourself in proximity to people that may connect with your vision.

Experts say that your audience needs six to twelve experiences seeing your name, product, or service to remember it exists. This can be an overwhelming thought. However, when you do it strategically, the cadence of your brand identity will start to seep into the DNA of those who need it the most.

Where Do You Begin?

So Many Ideas. So Much Opportunity. The good news is that there are a lot of avenues that you can utilize to spread the gospel of your fabulous new business. What is even better is that it doesn't have to be a huge financial investment. Although, I do believe in the old adage, "It takes money to make money." You can create a swirl of interest by using creativity and good, old-fashioned elbow grease.

Here is my go-to list that I use for my personal business and, in return, share with my clients.

CALL TO ACTION

Your call-to-action (CTA) is an important step of helping to turn coaching website visitors into paying clients. Without a clear call-to-action your website (and social media platforms) are just a place for people to find out about you and your services.

Here is a bit of information about me, here are the services that I offer, here is where you will find me—useful but not necessarily compelling enough for your visitor to want to take any kind of action. In order to have a website that works for your business you'll need to offer your would-be clients an obvious next step. Oftentimes, this comes in the form of a problem-solving headline and an action button.

Make it clear that you want to get them on the phone for a free, no-hassle discussion about their needs and your possible solutions. In addition, you want your CTA to do a number of things for you:

- Allow prospects to self-qualify.
- Gather key details from the prospect so you can do some vetting as well.
- Gauge their compatibility with your process and you as a coach.

WHAT IS YOUR CALL TO ACTION?

GETTING YOUR MESSAGE TO THE MASSES:

Website- Don't even think of launching without a website. Building a website that reflects your brand is the cornerstone of your business' visibility. Without a solid website, you will lose credibility and potential clients. This doesn't mean you have to spend thousands of dollars on a larger than life platform. It means that your brand needs to hold space on the internet as a reference for your customers. This is something you can do on your own or hire a professional. I am a self-taught web designer that explored various hosting sites until I got it right. My go-to website builder is **Wix.** It is user friendly and has a large variety of templates that you can choose from. If you are selling products, **Shopify** is a wonderful tool to display and sell your products. Other popular platforms are **Square Site, WordPress,** and **GoDaddy**. And if the mere mention of building your own website has you quaking in your boots, hire out a designer.

Don't be afraid to ask for help. I frequently dip into the freelancer pond when I am stuck or have limited time. Freelance designers flood sites like **Fiverr** and **Upwork.** Simply list your requirements and budget, and you will have experts knocking on your door. Find a designer who understands your vision, has excellent references, and has the time to walk you through the design process.

Launch Your Podcast- Launching a podcast can be a daunting idea. However, it is a powerful platform to facilitate the voice of your coaching business. Recently, I launched a podcast, "Obsessed With Humans On The Verge Of Change", and it has been met with accolades. There are opportunities to launch a podcast with little to no investment. You can also invest some capital and showcase a polished presentation of your coaching brand.

If your inclination is to play around with podcasting, start on **AnchorFM.** Anchor allows you to record and publish your program at no cost.

Podcasting expands the reach of your voice and your mission. It also adds a layer of credibility to your coaching business since it positions you as a thought leader and expert in your field.

Start Here

Anchor FM is a good (and free) place to start: www.anchor.fm Anchor is a free app that is super easy to navigate. You can record, edit and publish your podcast with ease.

Let me be clear, there is a lot that goes into producing a quality podcast. It is essential that you understand your voice and have the bandwidth to properly execute this project. The rewards of your efforts will pay back in dividends.

-->SEE THE PODCAST ADDENDUM FOR MORE INFORMATION ON LAUNCHING YOUR PODCAST.

CREATIVE WAYS TO BOOST VISABILITY

Think Outside the Box

Affiliations-Partner with similar businesses and team up to promote similar visions. This will exponentially increase the audience of both ventures.

Collaboration- The power of two doubles visibility. Find like-minded coaches who would love to collaborate on a project. You will gain visibility through their audience and vice versa.

I have worked in tandem with different coaches in various arenas. I have launched challenges, swapped content, and done promotions for other coaches. These connections will be an invaluable resource as you further your coaching career.

Online Course Creation- An online course is proof that you are an expert on a topic. There is no better way to gain notoriety as a thought leader than creating an online course.

Online Course Creator Tools

- Kajabi
- Teachable
- Thinkific
- Coursify

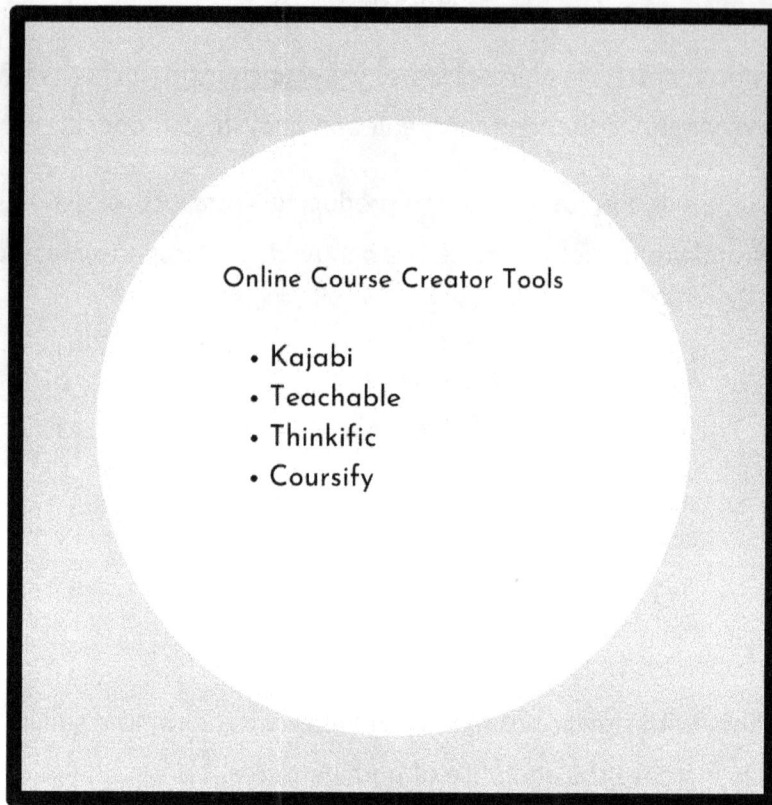

Swag- Everybody loves free stuff. Nothing gets the attention of a prospective client faster than a free t-shirt, hat, or notebook that is embroidered with your logo. Consider swag in your repertoire of visibility hacks. This is a critical yet straightforward cog in connecting with clients. It can be as simple as a business card or as elaborate as customized samples to give to your clients, pre-sale. It endears customers to your brand and is a reminder that they can't live without your service or product. Customized merch creates a brand presence and doesn't have to cost a fortune. My go-to favorite is **www.discountmugs.com.** I have used this site to customize mugs, pens, shirts, and journals. My clients are always giddy with excitement when they receive a personalized gift with a note that expresses my gratitude for their trust in me.

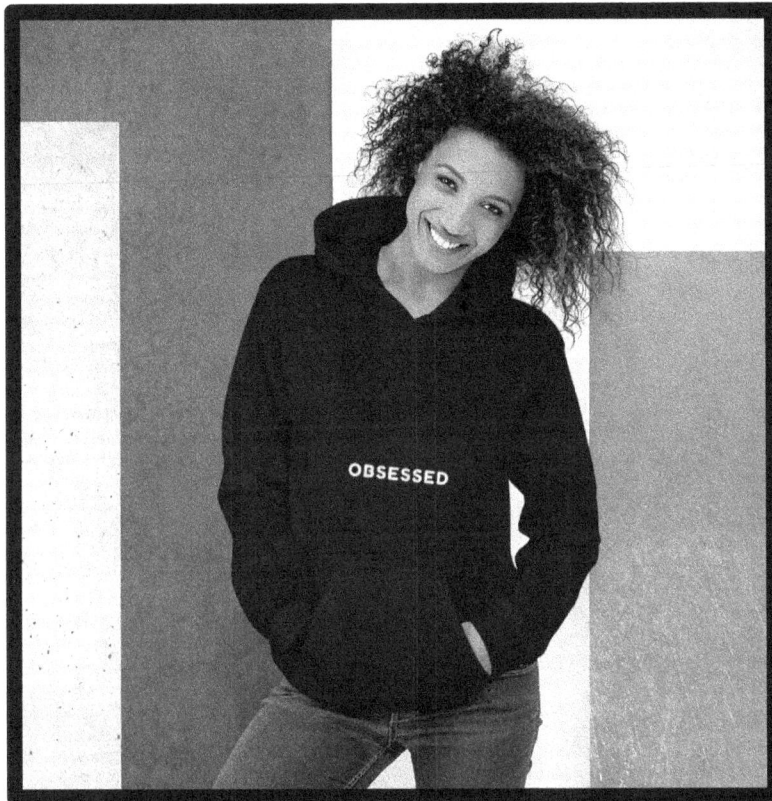

I am obsessed with **Printful.com.** It is an easy way to make a statement that your clients will remember. Printful is an on-demand printing and warehousing company that helps people turn their ideas into brands and products. Whether you wish to create your own online brand or give someone a personalized t-shirt, it's super easy to customize tee shirts, stickers, mugs and more. Printful is full service. They automatically receive the order, fulfill, and ship. You can literally do it in your sleep.

Free content-Creating visibility simply means sharing your vision. Free content is an extension of your vision and will create trust and a reputation with your future customers on an intimate level.

WHAT DOES FREE CONTENT MEAN?

I hear many experts exclaim, "Know your worth-don't give yourself and your services away for free." While I agree with the concept of understanding your self-worth, it is important, especially when you are starting off, that you work for free. This will establish you as a coach, and ultimately lead to referrals and reviews. The best part of offering services pro-bono is that you gain critical real-life coaching experience. Don't hold onto your services so tightly that no one is able to sample your expertise. The act of distributing free content sets the stage for establishing your reputation in the industry.

How To Offer Your Content For Free

- BLOGS
- FACEBOOK LIVES
- VIDEOS ON YOUTUBE
- E-BOOKS
- WEBINARS
- TUTORIALS
- 1:1 INTRODUCTORY SESSION/MEETING
- BOOKS
- SPEAKING ENGAGEMENTS
- LUNCH AND LEARNS
- SAMPLE OF PRODUCT

GROW YOUR REACH

Nourish the community you serve by getting involved.

Charitable partnerships-I champion every capable human to give their time, services, resources, and expertise to those in need. This philanthropic act should be executed with no intention other than to make the world a better place. The noble act of volunteering does have added benefits. You make connections, network, and allow people to witness your overall mission.

Contest or Challenge Pre-launch-This is a savvy entrepreneurial move to offer an attention-getting challenge. At the end of the challenge, offer a package or product to the grand-prize winner. Contests drum up unexpected excitement about your new business. It takes time to prepare and execute your pre-launch. However, when you emit extra energy, the enthusiasm is contagious. I offer challenges bi-yearly. Typically, they are five-day personal development challenges, and I award the winners with high price-point coaching packages worth nearly one thousand dollars. I don't approach my challenges with the mindset that I will make money due to my efforts. These challenges are launched to strategically expand my visibility and brand.

Free Coaching- Did I say free? Yes, free. Offer your service at no charge for a variety of reasons. Number 1 reason—you get experience. I truly believe in giving freely of my services—to a point. Especially when first starting out because it is great practice and provides the opportunity to serve. Double win!

YouTube Channel-Even if you aren't camera-ready, turn on your smartphone and give YouTube a try. Not only is **YouTube** a platform that garners increased visibility, but the website will also boost your rating on Google. **Google** is the gold standard of search engines. I believe that by harnessing the algorithms of this monolith, you will have clients flocking to your website.

GET SEEN

Paid Advertising-Google Ads-Google is an entity unlike any other. Whether you like it or not, it is a necessary evil. Dabble in **Google Ads.** You can pay as little as $3.00 a day to start creating a rhythm of website visitors. Don't dismiss the behemoth that is Google. Make friends with this search engine, because Google has the power to elevate your business or eliminate it.

THE POWER OF

⊕INTEREST

Pinterest- (I'm obsessed with the sleeping giant.) Don't be fooled by this unassuming powerhouse of a search engine. Yes, I said search engine. Many users are misinformed about Pinterest's power, and they often label it "social media." I'm obsessed with this platform since it is Google in disguise. Pinterest attracts users that are in the discovery phase of a search. Users are looking for recipes, or clothing, and even inspiration in their lives. And, the amazing part of the user experience is that users are poised to purchase.

The algorithms are such that content can be used and reused, unlike social media platforms. The Pinterest algorithm soaks up current pins. For example, if it is February, pins that smack of love and Valentine's tend to garner more interest.

How do you start on Pinterest? Use your **Canva** account to create appealing visuals that aren't blatant advertisements. First, think about your desired audience and ask yourself, *what would this audience be interested in?* My desired audience is interested in personal and professional development, so they are most likely drawn to words of inspiration and personal growth tips.

Don't make your pin specific to a sale or advertisement. Draw in your audience with a visually appealing display of something you represent. For example, a client who happens to own a bakery should post a recipe or a photo of a decadent pastry. This expands visibility.

Remember, visibility is the key to establishing your brand.

Why Pinterest Works

When you draw a client in with your vibrant pin, you have the opportunity to expand on this pin in your content. When a user clicks on the pin, it immediately takes them to your website. This provides a one-step process. A photo and simple content attract a user; then, they are swept to your website, where you can elaborate on your life-altering product or service. The simple 1-click step of getting a user to your website will lead to client engagement and a possible sale. (Remember, simple is better. The more a user is required to navigate different platforms, the more likely you will lose their attention.)

What's even better?

If a Pinterest user pins one of your pins to their board, all of their followers will experience your brand. Pinterest has the capability to expand your visibility exponentially.

Hustler's Tip: Budget a little money to invest in **Pinterest Ads.** You can budget as little as two dollars a day, and your pins will be seen. My website hits doubled in the first week of testing out this marketing strategy.

*The demographics of Pinterest are 80% women who possess untapped buying potential. I typically curate my pins to be female-centric.

Press Release-Sharpen your Number 2 pencil and start writing. Write a short snippet on why your business will change the world. Remember, it must be newsworthy, so craft a vignette of why it is crucial that the community learns of your work. Once all the T's are crossed and the I's are dotted, search local papers, magazines, and media outlets that may be interested in your story. Look for a page on their website that allows for press release submissions. Send your story their way and sit back and wait for your inbox to start clamoring for more! Press Releases are another amazing vehicle to gain visibility and boost your ranking in Google.

Hustler's Tip: I use EIN Presswire to distribute releases. With one click of the mouse, your press release will be sent to dozens of media outlets. www.einpresswire.com

Podcast Pitches- Ask yourself, what podcasts your potential customers listen to. Once you have narrowed down a list of podcasts, email them the undeniable reasons they should feature you. Make this pitch short and poignant. Distinguish yourself as a leader in the industry and be very clear about why you will empower their audience. Add links to your website, press, and anything powerful that states that you are a credible thought leader in this niche. Remember to make your contact information easily accessible so they can reach out with one click. Also, keep it brief.

Checkout Pitch Podcasts: www.pitchpodcasts.com

New Episode

OBSESSED

with perfection

BE BRAVE & KIND

Be The Voice That Changes The World
Learn More About Julie Lokun + The Obsessed Podcast

SIMPLIFYING SEO MANAGEMENT

SEO/ Search Engine Optimizations- Are inextricably linked to brand visibility. The topic of **SEOs** is complex, yet so simple. Figure out what your potential client will type in a search engine to find your business. Once you have tapped into your future client's mind, use these keywords in all the content you produce. For example, smatter these keywords all over your website. Sprinkle them in your social media, in your press releases, and everything you send out into cyberspace.

SEO BRAINSTORM- What search words will your potential client google to find you?

_____

_____

_____

My go too app for SEOs- KEYWORDS EVERYWHERE.

Keywords Everywhere is a Chrome Extension App (Google) that finds powerful keywords and provides tools to optimize your brand on Google. It is imperative that you curate keywords that are highly searched but have limited competition. It is priced at a relatively low ($10) price point and has been a game changer in my SEO repertoire.

HUSTLER TIPS-

Brainstorm keywords and phrases. Keywords are the words on your website that people are most likely to search for. Brainstorm several options related to the theme of your website. Businesses may want to conduct market research or run a focus group to help this process along. If you're starting a website on a small budget, just have a brainstorm session by yourself or with a few friends.

- If you'll be writing about products, search for similar products on online marketplaces. Look for common phrases in the product names and descriptions.

- Search for online forums related to your website topic. Read through some of the post titles and popular discussions to find topics of interest.

NOTES:

_____

_____

_____

_____

_____

_____

_____

CLUBHOUSE: THE SECRET WEAPON FOR COACHES

I'm addicted to this new platform that serves up true connections, limitless networking possibilities, and provides the opportunity to grow and expand my mind daily. **Clubhouse** is non-negotiable for coaches who want to network, collaborate and grow their base. I can say with unabashed certainty that you, as a coach, need to utilize this up-and-coming platform.

WHAT THE HECK IS CLUBHOUSE?

Clubhouse is an audio-only social media app known for its unconstrained conversations, celebrity backers, and invite-only status. The experience falls somewhere between call-in radio and professional conference. Users select rooms based on interest, then engage in live conversation. Room moderators decide who speaks, and it's common to see rooms with dozens of active participants. The still-in-beta app exploded in popularity at the start of 2021, reaching eight million downloads by mid-February despite limiting enrollment. Currently, the app is in beta testing and the full launch is planned later in 2021.

Clubhouse, in my opinion, is **LinkedIn** on steroids. While LinkedIn has its place in navigating job searches, LinkedIn user engagement seems dormant. Specifically, LinkedIn is used on an as-needed basis. (I need a job, so I need to check out LinkedIn).

Clubhouse, on the other hand, is a space that expands user experience by providing instant gratification. Clubhouse has provided the ground floor for job hires, shark-tank life investments, and intimate conversations to take place. This app is known for its lightning bolt conversations that facilitate networking on a scale nowhere else seen.
The Proof.
My two weeks journey on Clubhouse has resulted in:

- Collaborations with influential humans that inspire others to be bold and live outside the box.
- A shared space to meditate. Yes! They have rooms for meditation.
- An increase in client engagement.
- An increase in my knowledge base of things I am passionate about: personal development, health and wellness, personal branding, self-actualization and much more.
- Helped me fine-tune my public speaking skills.

- Introduced me, and provided unprecedented access to influential public figures who have agreed to be guests on my podcast, "Obsessed, With Humans On The Verge Of Change."

- Daily inspiration to do better and be better.

The best part of Clubhouse is that, when you join, you have access to limitless brain power. You are able to listen to live conversations on almost any topic. You can join the conversation and ask questions, or pick the brains of prolific thought leaders.
If this isn't enough, you can moderate your own rooms, choose the topic of conversation, and invite others to join in on impactful subject matter.

WHO SHOULD JOIN CLUBHOUSE?

All coaches should do this. Now! You should dip your toe in the Clubhouse pond and start sharing your story.

WHERE DO YOU START?

Because it is in beta testing, it is invite-and can be accessed through your phone.
The rumor is that the android version of Clubhouse will be available this fall.

Download the Clubhouse App to sign up. It may take a while to be admitted because the app creators want to keep a controlled flow of users. Or, find a friend on Clubhouse and ask them to invite you. Clubhouse users are allotted a managed amount of invites, which they can send to their friends.

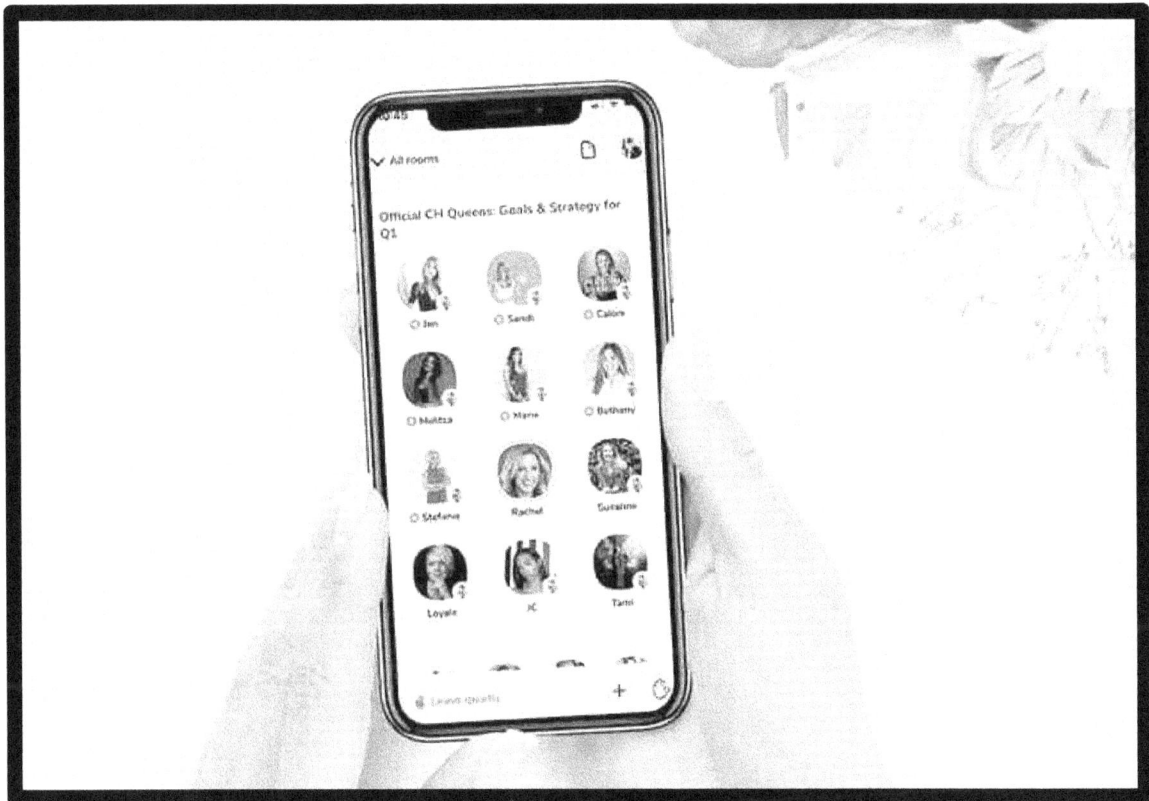

Next, play around with the app. Visit different rooms, listen in on the conversations. Join the conversation or better yet, be the conversation. Enjoy the interactive experience and be inspired daily by a cross-section of perspectives.

VISIBILITY REVISITED

To start your brand-spanking-new business, you must create a vision for your brand, and how you will represent this brand to the world is critical. Elevating this vision to capture the imagination of a targeted audience can be a labor of love. The visibility pillar will establish you in the game. Visibility is a consistent cadence of creatively thinking outside the box. Start small and don't give up.

The process of establishing a visible brand will distinguish you from your competitors. This process allows for trial and error, so dabble in different exercises and position your ideas on various platforms. Remember, it takes time to start seeing results, but when you do, it is the sweetest validation of your hard work.

NOTES:

_____

_____

_____

_____

_____

_____

_____

SOCIAL MEDIA -A NECESSARY EVIL?

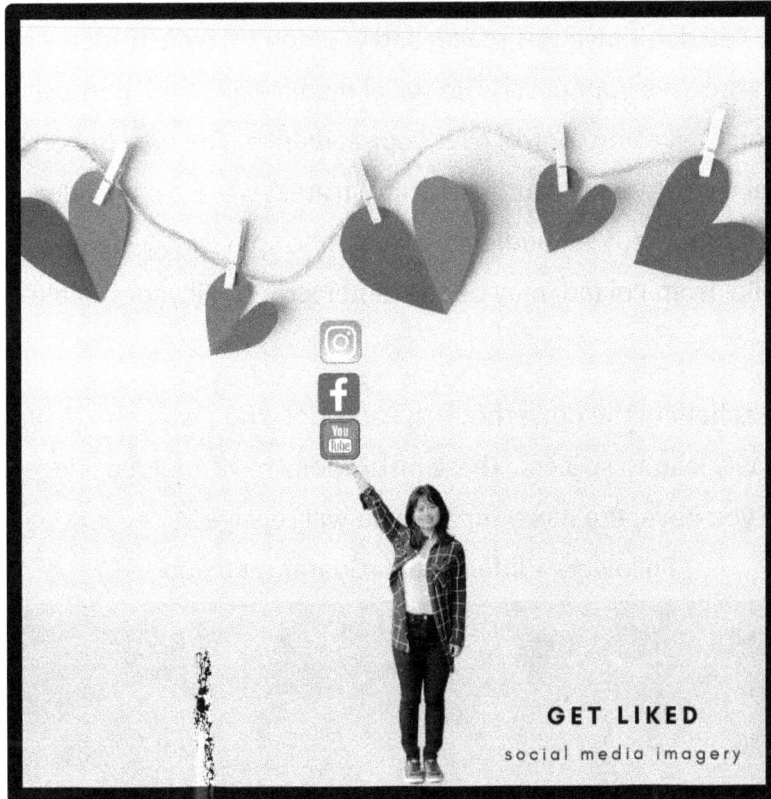

GET LIKED

social media imagery

Social media is a misunderstood spot in cyberspace. My experience on the biggies, Facebook, Instagram and Twitter has been an energy-sucking vortex of confusion with the addictive need to be liked and followed. I understand the draw to these powerful institutions. However, I stand firmly rooted in the fact that social media disempowers your marketing efforts. Social media is an illusion. This illusion is a carousel of momentary images that induce feelings of self-doubt and comparison. At an organic level, social media is a fabulous touch point to connect with long-lost friends. It allows you to share and catalog special moments. However, I feel strongly that social media is not the forum to sell your goods, but it is an excellent platform to establish your online presence.

This, perhaps, is a confusing message. A common misconception about social media is that this is a platform to sell yourself. The truth is that the number of followers, likes, and heart emojis do not easily convert into sales. Social media is akin to marketing on borrowed land. You don't own this space, and you don't have any idea who sees your posts and when they see your posts. The social media algorithm, purposefully, remains a mystery. You don't have any control over your audience. The idea of borrowed-land in regards to social media means your marketing strategies are a crapshoot. Visibility is not guaranteed. What's more, your audience may not be specifically curated to your message. So, Filip, from Poland, may be the benefactor of all your female-inspired make-up tips.

The masterminds behind the powerhouses, Facebook and Instagram, have you believing that their tools will lead to success. These institutions have wielded a legend that the more followers you have, the more success you will receive.

Followers = Influencer = Guaranteed Success

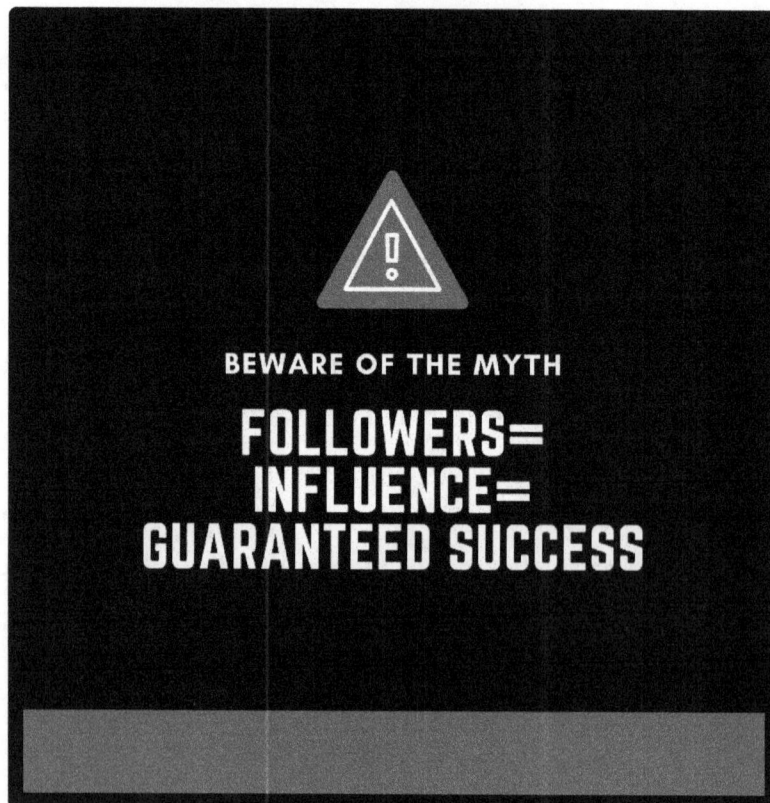

BEWARE OF THE MYTH

FOLLOWERS=
INFLUENCE=
GUARANTEED SUCCESS

This line of thought can be rebutted by the fact that a mass following dilutes your message. Again, I emphasize that prioritizing your marketing efforts solely on social media is like marketing on borrowed land. When you have collected a large following, your audience spans many demographics, and many of these followers won't have an interest in your service or product. Coupled with this, the mysterious algorithms of Facebook and Instagram and the impact of your marketing strategies are left to the whims of the wizard behind the curtain.

If social media is a vortex of unpredictable exposure to a slightly interested audience, how can you firmly expand your visibility on solid ground?

Refer to the list above. Pique the interest of the audience who sits at the feet of your wisdom. And don't forget the almighty email list. The **email list** is the mightiest form of delivering impactful content to an audience who is already interested in you.

SO, WHY USE SOCIAL MEDIA

Admittedly, I have painted a negative image of social media. And the truth is, I have Facebook and Instagram accounts. These two polarizing stances don't seem to make sense at first. To clarify, social media is an excellent platform to establish visibility. Social media is an ideal platform to tell your story; however, it is not the place to sell.

Social media is a laser-focused tool for you to use in your business strategy. Layer posts with gorgeous illustrations of what you do and what you love.

Instagram is a place where you can send out a polished snapshot of your accomplishments. Curate your brand and create a call to action. Engagement with followers is essential to really create trust. A streamlined instagram account will catch the attention of potential clients and like minded entrepreneurs.

Facebook is the perfect platform for you to engage future clients by hosting a group or a page. I won't minimize the power of Facebook to engage your clients. It's a useful tool to create space for like-minded seekers of your information.

With Facebook, you can launch live broadcasts and speak on a soapbox. This allows you to create an authentic relationship with your audience and gain a sense of trust. Their curiosity will lead them to your website. And your website will illustrate your talents further. Ideally, your website will captivate this audience and transcend these users into devoted fans. Your website is where the magic happens.

Make sure you are consistent with your posts and have a call to action.

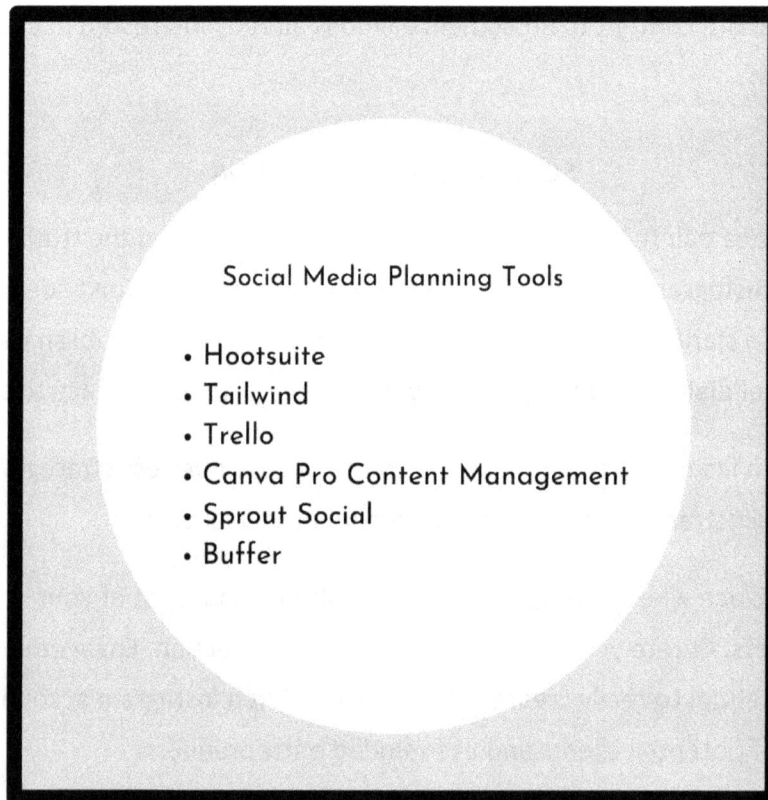

Social Media Planning Tools

- Hootsuite
- Tailwind
- Trello
- Canva Pro Content Management
- Sprout Social
- Buffer

MONTHLY MARKETING PLAN
MONTH:
BUDGET:

	WEEK 1	WEEK 2	WEEK 3	WEEK 4
MON				
TUE				
WED				
THU				
FRI				

@HUSTLE SMART FOR COACHES

WEEKLY SOCIAL MEDIA PLANNER

Instagram | Facebook
Pinterest| LinkedIn | Twitter

WEEK OF:
CALL TO ACTION:

MONDAY	TUESDAY
☐	☐
☐	☐
☐	☐
☐	☐

WEDNESDAY	THURSDAY
☐	☐
☐	☐
☐	☐
☐	☐

FRIDAY	SATURDAY
☐	☐
☐	☐
☐	☐
☐	☐

SUNDAY	SOMETIME THIS WEEK
☐	☐
☐	☐
☐	☐
☐	☐

HustleSmart For Coaches ©

ADDENDUM:

CREATING A PODCAST YOU LOVE

PODCASTING FOR BEGINNERS: Hustle Smart Podcasting Addendum

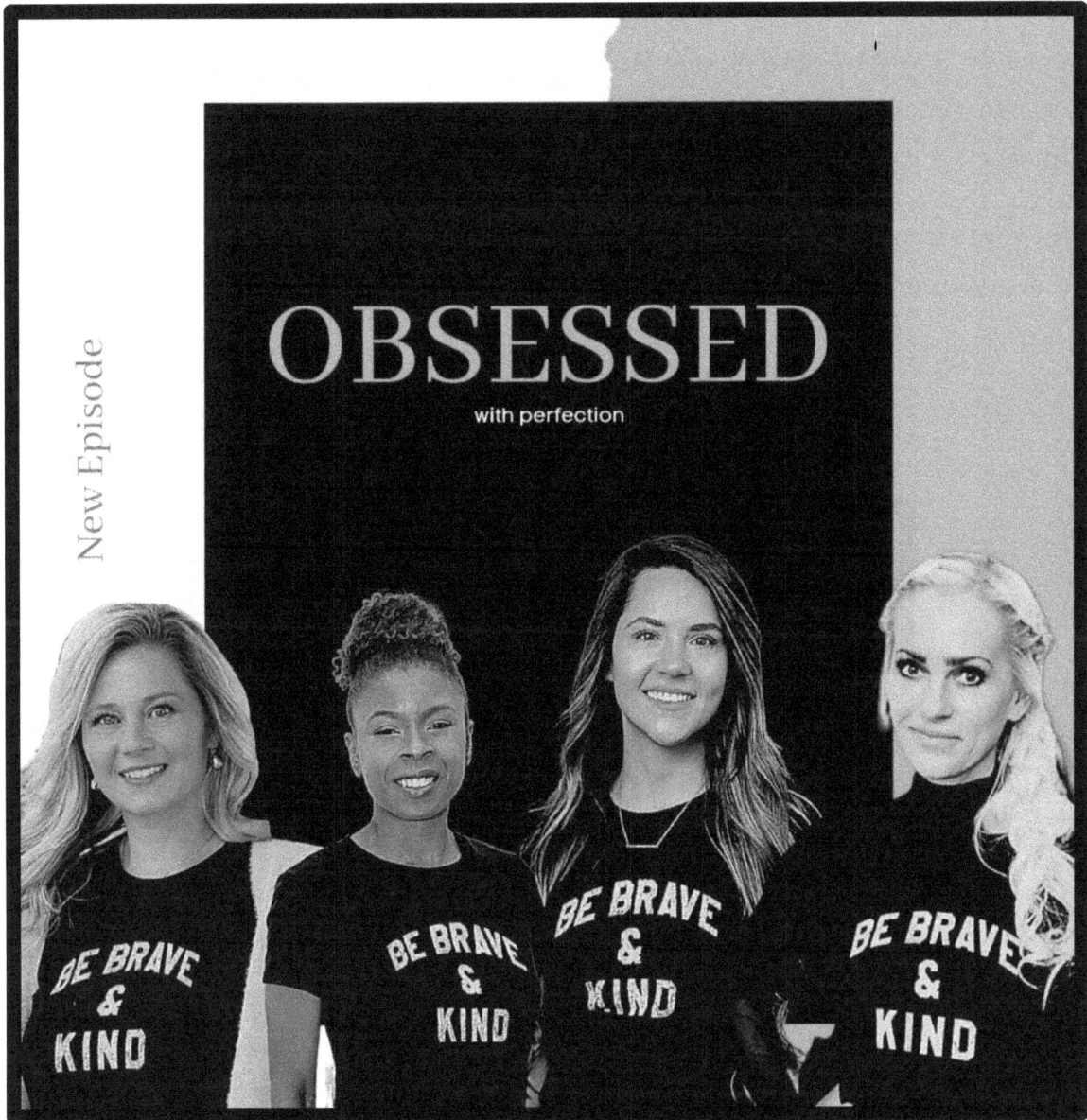

EXPAND THE BRAND YOU LOVE

If you have ever considered launching your own podcast, I would encourage you to play around with the idea. It has been a wonderful extension of my brand and I have the opportunity to help so many more people.

A podcast is a digital audio file that you can stream from the internet or download and listen to. Podcasts can be free or sold for a fee. You can set up a podcasting site or "channel" and make daily podcasts like a radio show.

The key to launching a successful podcast is consistency. Consistent episode drops will ensure you engage a regular audience. Most podcasts do not make it past 6 episodes.

REASONS TO CONSIDER PODCASTING

YOUR POTENTIAL AUDIENCE IS LISTENING WHEN THEY:

- Work out
- Wash the dishes
- Take a walk
- Mow the grass
- Drive
- Sit in a bus or train
- Vacuum the carpet
- Sit by the pool

1. **20% of adults report listening to podcasts at least occasionally.** That's a lot of people you can reach with your voice!

2. **Podcasting is much less crowded than blogging.** The blogging landscape is very crowded. Get out of that space and consider starting a podcast, instead.

3. **There is more intimacy.** The written word is no substitute for the spoken word. With a podcast, you can connect on a whole new level.

4. **You can reach a new crowd.** Many people won't read a blog, but will listen to a podcast.

Podcasting has many advantages over the other forms of online marketing. **You can provide value in a new and more meaningful way.** Podcasting is even easier than blogging, because you don't need a website to get started.

GETTING STARTED WITH PODCASTING

You can get started quickly with only a couple of tools:

1. **A quality microphone.** Fortunately, a good microphone is only around $50. *The Snowball by Blue Microphones is the most popular.* I also like the brand **Audio Technica**. Do a little research and find a quality microphone. Remember that you're only recording your voice. You don't need a microphone that can handle the crushing volume of a drum set.

In a pinch, a combination headset-microphone can work well enough to get started. Move up to a better microphone when your finances allow.

The headset combo is also a good option if you're interviewing others. Remember that you have to be able to hear the other person without the sound spilling over into your microphone.

2.**A computer to store the recordings.** Actually, there are many alternatives to a computer, but you'll need a computer to upload your podcast anyway.

That's all you need to get started. There's no excuse! *A simple microphone and your computer are all you need to make a high quality podcast.* Start looking for a microphone today. You can produce your first podcast immediately.

A FEW TOP HOSTING SITES

PodBean

Lisbyn

Anchor FM

Buzz Sprout

Captivate

Essentials For Podcast Launch
- Artwork
- Format + Style
- Trailer Episode
- Show Notes
- Royalty-Free Music Clips
- RSS Feed

CREATING YOUR FIRST PODCAST

Just Do It! Start Recording! You can record from your phone, your computer, Zoom or Riverside-just to name a few. Remember the quality of the sound is the most important element of your podcast.

If your sound is tinny or muffled-it will automatically turn listeners off. Your raw audio file must be in an MP3 file format to upload to your hosting site.

1. **Choose a format.** There are a few ways to conduct your podcast:

Go solo

Have one or more guests

Most podcasters stick to a single format and occasionally change it up. Your listeners will probably grow to expect and like a particular format, but don't be afraid to vary it on occasion.

 2. **Prepare.** Unless you're very talented, you'll want notes, and perhaps, a full script. If you're interviewing someone, have questions ready.

Consider the purpose of the podcast. What are you trying to share, teach, or explain? Perhaps your podcast is strictly for entertainment purposes.

 3. **Record in a quiet space.** People don't enjoy listening to anything with a lot of background noise. It's distracting and shows a lack of professionalism.

4. **Edit appropriately.** There are many audio programs available for cutting and pasting sections of your podcast. Many of them are free. Ensure that any guests who participate in your podcast have the opportunity to review your edits before making the podcast public.

What could be easier? It can be a little more intimidating to put your voice online than writing a blog post. But that also makes it more effective. You're putting a part of yourself out there for the world to experience.

Once you've recorded your podcast, it's time to make it available to others.

Getting Your Podcast Out to the Masses

SENDING OUT YOUR PODCAST

1. **Create an RSS feed.** You can upload your podcast to a single site and it will automatically be delivered to your subscribers.

2. **Use iTunes.** iTunes will deliver your podcast to subscribers, and people will be able to search for it. You can choose whether or not to charge a fee.

After uploading to iTunes, you can expect it will take approximately 5-7 days until your podcast is available because there is a review process.

3. **Upload your podcast to other sites. Soundcloud** is a popular platform and provides multiple sharing options.

4. **Use social media.** Tell everyone about your latest podcast. Get every listener you can find. They're all potential customers.

Use your imagination. Market your podcast any way you can. Every loyal listener is potentially another dollar in your pocket. Marketing is the key.

Now that you have a podcast and listeners, the next step is monetization. It's time to boost your income.

MAKING MONEY WITH YOUR PODCAST

1. **Sell your own products.** Do you have a course or other product for sale? You can use your podcast to promote your products. The show can be about your product, or you can casually mention it during the show. In your podcast, entice people to visit your website where they can buy your products.

2. **Sell affiliate products.** Don't have any of your own products? Sell someone else's. This is a great way to lure guests to your show. Let them tell your audience all about their life-changing doo-dad. You can take a piece of the action with an affiliate commission.

3. **Sell your podcast.** You can also charge for your podcast. Some podcasters put out a few free episodes and then sell the rest. Some make a short version available free of charge but charge a fee for the full episode.

4. **Charge for advertising.** Make money by charging other companies for advertising on your show. This works especially well when you've built an audience. Find companies who sell products to your target audience. Run a prerecorded commercial or promote the company in the context of your show.

There are other ways to make money with your podcast. Find sponsors. Get donations. Use the podcast to build your brand and market your services. **Whenever you have an audience, the possibility for making money exists.** The possibilities are only limited by your imagination!

Consider podcasting as a means to boost your income. There are a lot of ways to monetize your podcasts. All you need is a microphone, computer, and a little free time. Provide true value, and the money will follow.

THE HUSTLE SMART PODCAST LAUNCH CHECKLIST:

 Requirements To Start Podcasting-

1. Subscribe to a Podcast Hosting Site like Anchor FM or Lisbyn
Email/Username: _____
Password: _____

I highly recommend the Advanced 400 Plan of Libsyn which already includes analytics reporting. AnchorFM, BuzzSprout, Captivate, and Wondery are good options as well.

2. Dedicated Email Address
Email:
Password:
For podcast use only. This dedicated email address is to set up the podcast channels and tools.

3. Log-in Credentials for Apple (Apple ID)
Apple ID: _____
Password: _____
The hosting site will need to be connected to your Apple ID.
I will need to submit the show to Apple for approval.

4. Source Music and Sound Effects
Link: Email/Username:
Password:

To avoid legal problems in the future, I highly recommend getting a paid musician or check out my list below!

5. Intro audio recording.
Create an elevator pitch or benefits that the listeners will get from the show.
You may hire voice talent for this or you can record your own.

6. Outro audio recording
What is your Call To Action?
You may hire voice talent for this or you can record your own.

7. Shared Repository or Storage if you are Co-Hosting or Have A Producer
(Google Drive Recommended)
Link:
Email/Username:_____
Password:_____
We can use DropBox or Google Drive. Please provide access.
It's highly recommended that we have a single location for all assets and
files (audios, music, and documents)

8. Trailer Episode audio recording- Post a trailer episode 2-3 weeks prior to
the launch. The trailer length should be 3-5 minutes long.

Your About Episode:
Let your listeners know they are in the right place and what will they get
every time they tune in.

9. 1 Pilot Episode audio recording
This will be the first podcast episode.

format with appropriate file extensions.

Priority Requirements	Remarks
1. Subscribe to a Podcast Hosting Email/Username: Password:	I highly recommend the *Advanced 400 Plan* of Libsyn which already includes analytics reporting. AnchorFM, BuzzSprout, Captivate and Wondery are good options as well.
2. Dedicated Email Address Email: Password:	• For podcast use only. This dedicated email address is to set-up the podcast channels and tools.
3. Log-in Credentials for Apple (Apple ID) Apple ID: _____ Password: _____	• The hosting site will need to be connected to your Apple ID. • I will need to submit the show to Apple for approval.
4. Source Music and Sound Effects Link: Email/Username: Password:	• To avoid legal problems in the future, I highly recommend getting a paid musician.
5. Intro audio recording	• *Elevator pitch or benefits* that the listeners will get from the show. • You may hire *voice talent* for this or you can record your own.
6. Outro audio recording	• *What is your Call To Action?* • You may hire *voice talent* for this or you can record your own.

7. Shared Repository or Storage if Co-Hosting or Have A Producer (Google Drive Recommended) Link: Email/Username: Password:	• We can use *DropBox* or *Google Drive*. Please provide access. • It's highly recommended that we have a single location for all assets and files (audios, music, and documents)
8. Trailer Episode audio recording- Post a trailer episode 2-3 weeks prior to the launch. The trailer length should be 3-5 minutes long.	• Your About Episode • Let your listeners know they are in the right place and what will they get every time they tune in.
9. 1 Pilot Episode audio recording	• This will be the first podcast episode.

Podcast Show Requirements	Remarks
Your Podcast Name/Show Title	Chose Something That Stands Out
Podcast Description	<ul><li>AKA show summary, why they should listen & what can they expect.</li><li>Limit to 2-3 sentences only.</li></ul>
Show Category:	<ul><li>Here's a guide: https://podcasts.apple.com/us/genre/podcasts/id26</li></ul>
Authors	<ul><li>AKA the host(s) of the podcast show</li></ul>
Keywords	Curate a list of keywords that spell out
Podcast artwork (please observe image requirements to prevent the show from getting rejected by Apple/iTunes). Link:	<ul><li>[**Cover art** must be] a minimum size of 1400 x 1400 pixels and a maximum size of 3000 x 3000 pixels, 72 dpi, in JPEG or PNG format with appropriate file extensions.</li></ul>

THE HUSTLE SMART PODCAST LAUNCH CHECKLIST:

The Hustle Smart Brainstorm:

Name Of Podcast:

Genre Of Podcast:

Key Words

List Of Topics:

Compiled List of Resources For Launching your Podcast:

Anchor FM- Free Hosting App

Apple For Podcast Creators- Upload and monetize your podcast.

Audacity- Audio Editor

Audio Jungle- Royalty Free Music Clips

Audrey.io- Collaborate with other podcasters

BuzzSprout- Hosting App

Canva - Create Podcast Artwork

Captivate - Hosting App

Chartable- Podcast Ranking Resource

Epidemic Sound- Royalty Free Music Clips

LinkTree- One stop site for all your links

Libsyn - Hosting Apps

Pitch Podcasts - Pitch yourself to other podcasters

Riverside FM- Hosting Site and Recording Site

Zoom- Record your episodes and download audio file

More Questions?
Sign Up For A Free 25-Minute
Podcasting Strategy Session
julie@julielokuncoaching.com

⚓ **Notes & Take-Aways:**

THE ULTIMATE GUIDE FOR NEW ENTREPRENUERS

HUSTLE
SMART©

JULIE LOKUN

Facilitate Your Dreams. Learn How To Launch Your Idea Into A Thriving Business.

www.ingramcontent.com/pod-product-compliance
Lightning Source LLC
Chambersburg PA
CBHW082059210326
41521CB00032B/2513